Aberdeenshire Library and Information Service
www.aberdeenshire.gov.uk/alis
Renewals Hotline 01224 661511

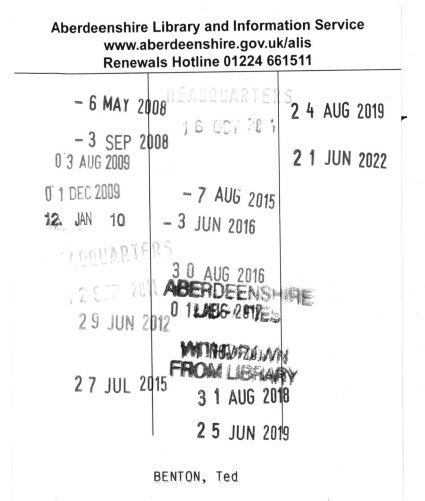
BENTON, Ted

The easy
butterfly guide

Common Blue

The Easy Butterfly Guide

Britain and Europe

Written and photographed by **Ted Benton**
Paintings by **Tim Bernhard**

Red Admiral

First published in Great Britain by Aurum Press Ltd
25 Bedford Avenue, London WC1B 3AT

© Duncan Petersen Publishing Ltd 2006

ISBN 1-84513-120-7

Printed by Fotolito Star, Italy

Conceived, edited, designed and produced by Duncan Petersen Publishing:
C7, Old Imperial Laundry, Warriner Gardens, London SW11 4XW

Editors Helen Warren and Hermione Edwards
Designer Ian Midson
Editorial director Andrew Duncan
Photography by Ted Benton
Paintings by Tim Bernhard

Foreword

Encounters with butterflies are among my earliest memories: clusters of red admirals, peacocks and small tortoiseshells on buddleia blossom in a churchyard; finding the chrysalids of large whites attached to the wall of my primary school; common blues and brown arguses in a flowery field near our family home. My parents encouraged the interest, and bought me the invaluable *Observer's* book, then Edmund Sandars' *A Butterfly Book for the Pocket.* In those days, many of the butterflies that are now vanishing rarities were quite common and widespread. But even then, there were almost mythical species, ones that appeared on the colour plates of the books, or museum cabinets, but seemed for ever out of reach. Would I ever see a purple emperor, a silver-spotted skipper or an adonis blue?

Since then, greater mobility, and still more books, have opened up the wider compass of continental Europe. With somewhere near 400 species to find, study and photograph, this has turned into a life-long project. For many years, family holidays were planned around likely butterfly possibilities, and Shelley, Jay and Rowan have my thanks (and apologies) for putting up with my sudden disappearance after some nondescript little brown butterfly. Soon, of course, the obsession got too demanding to be contained in the family holiday, and annual field excursions had to be carefully planned with target species in mind. Lacking a really suitable starter guide-book, we were fortunate enough to have the help and guidance of numerous fellow enthusiasts: Joe Firmin, Ronnie Leestmans, Nils Ryrholm, Claes Eliasson, Tristan Lafranchis, Tom Tolman, David Jutzeler, Miguel Munguira, Helmut Höttinger, Stanislav Abadjiev, Peter Russell, Basil Yates-Smith and many others. My companions on many field trips over 25 years – Bernard Watts, Vic Barnham, John Kramer, Simon Randolph, Andrew Wakeham-Dawson, Roland Rogers, Tama Hacs, 'Stepan' and many others from across Europe – have shared some unforgettable adventures.

Finally, it has been a pleasure and an honour to work with Tim Bernhard in the preparation of this book: his paintings speak for themselves – among the finest I've seen. He wishes to express his gratitude to his grandfather for understanding and encouraging his love of nature, and for many happy hours spent in the field. He would also like to acknowledge the help given by Dr. Christopher Luckens.

Sooty Copper

Contents

THE METALMARKS

THE NYMPHALIDS, FRITILLARIES AND BROWNS

THE SKIPPERS

About this book

Adonis Blue

CAN THE IDENTIFICATION AND STUDY OF BUTTERFLIES BE MADE EASY?
The honest answer has to be 'no': **BUT** it can be made less difficult. This guide aims to give you a reader-friendly introduction to what can become a whole lifetime of fascination.

HOW?
●**A manageable number of species, carefully selected.** Europe is home to approximately 400 kinds of butterflies. A fully comprehensive butterfly guide is needed for those who go on to make a special lifelong study of butterflies, but it can be very confusing for the beginner to see pages of apparently identical specimens. In fact, many kinds of butterfly are limited to very small areas - in a few cases to just one mountain - and will not be discovered without a great deal of effort. So, most butterfly watchers, and especially beginners, need a book that covers only those species that are likely to be seen.

●**But the selection has to be carefully made:** too many butterfly books feature rare and exotic species because they are eye-catching, even though they are not likely to be seen by the reader. The butterflies selected for treatment in this book include those that are widespread throughout Europe, but also some that are more localised, but quite common and easily found within their local range. To make the selection feasible, the geographical focus of the book has been confined to western-central and northern European countries. This means that some butterflies that occur only in Greece and the Balkans, or in only Italy, Spain and Portugal have been omitted. However, the book should still be useful even in those parts of Europe, and will enable identification of most butterflies you are likely to see.

●**Clear photos and paintings:** each species is illustrated by a vivid photograph taken of a living butterfly in its natural habitat. Unlike illustrations of dead, set specimens, this gives you the view of the butterfly as you will encounter it in the wild. On the opposite page you will find specially commissioned paintings that give you an alternative view of the butterfly, or, where the sexes are different, the opposite sex. The paintings are also used to illustrate details needed to be sure of your identification, and to show early stages in the butterfly's life history. Each species has a European distribution map and a silhouette showing its actual size.

●**More information, clearly expressed:** the text and captions for each species tell you the best places and times to see it, details of its life history, how it spends the winter and any other aspects of interest. Where possible, technical terms have been avoided, but some are useful, and their meaning is explained at the end of this introduction.

How to use this book

In order to identify a butterfly, a random search through the pages, scanning the pictures, should give you the answer in most cases. However, a much better short-cut is to take the trouble to learn the different families and groups of butterflies: so, if you know you have a blue or a fritillary you can go directly to that section of the book. In the sub-section on classification, below, we explain these sub-divisions among the butterflies. When you have found the illustration that most closely fits the appearance of the butterfly you are trying to identify, check the lookalikes section of the text, and also look to see if there are paintings of distinguishing details. For more reassurance you can check the information given in the text about its flight period and the distribution map. In most cases you can be quite confident that you have the right species. However, there are a few groups that include many similar species, so that all we can do in this guide is to show some distinctive examples. The Mountain Ringlets are one such group, with more than 40 European species: identifying some of these can be a problem even for experts.

But this guide is meant to be much more than a guide to identifying butterflies. Every species is the unique outcome of millions of years of evolution, during which time it has become adapted to its environment: behaviour, colour pattern, life history, the feeding patterns of the caterpillars and so on can be related to its survival in its preferred habitat. In some cases (such as the Large Blue) this involves very specialised adaptations, such as the secretion of sugar to attract the protection of a particular species of red ant. At the opposite extreme, butterflies such as the Small Tortoiseshell and Large White lay their eggs on very common plants, and can be found almost anywhere in towns or countryside. The text and paintings are designed to give you a deeper understanding of the butterfly that you have identified, and at least begin to explain some of these features of its way of life.

Key identifying features and details of early stages in the life-cycle. **These paintings are not always lifesize – the size key below gives exact butterfly dimensions.**

Size key gives exact sizes of butterflies.

Ted Benton's photographs show the butterfly's overall appearance, brilliantly capturing how it strikes the eye in the wild.

Captions describe the diagnostic points in simple language.

Main text describes the habitat and feeding patterns as well as different stages of the butterfly's development.

Map showing range. Captions beneath give extra detail on where and when the species occur.

Introduction to butterflies and how to study them

ANATOMY OF A BUTTERFLY

Butterflies belong to a much bigger order of insects, the Lepidoptera (literally: scale-wings), which includes both butterflies and moths. On the global scale, there are no sharp distinctions between butterflies and moths. In some countries the two groups are distinguished as night-flyers and day-flyers, and this works quite well. However, there are quite a few kinds of moth that fly in daylight, and some of these (for example the burnets) are also brightly coloured like

Clouded yellow

many butterflies. In Europe, there are several other features you can use to distinguish butterflies from moths. The butterflies are usually distinguished from moths by the shape of the antennae ('feelers'). These are widened towards the end to give a club-like appearance in butterflies, whilst the antennae of moths are variously shaped, often simple and thread-like, or feathery. Usually moths rest with wings folded down over and beside their bodies, whilst butterflies close their wings up above their bodies. A less obvious characteristic is that moths have tiny 'hooks' linking fore- and hind-wings, which butterflies lack. The skipper butterflies have quite furry bodies and look moth-like. Some writers do not count them as butterflies, but we include some representative species in this guide. In addition to the skippers, we include examples of five other families - see below under Classification.

Perhaps the reason why butterflies are so popular (apart from the fact that they don't sting or bite) is the astonishing diversity of colour and patterning on their wings. As the scientific name of the order to which they belong suggests, these colours are produced by tiny scales which cover both surfaces of the wings like fine dust (which rubs off when a butterfly is worn with age or handled carelessly). In most cases, the colour patterns result from the mosaic of pigments on the scales, but in some species (especially the blues) iridescent colours are produced by the refraction of light through the scales. Quite recently, scientific studies with ultraviolet light have shown patterns, probably important in butterfly courtship and mating, which are not visible to the human eye. As well as playing their part in recognition for courtship and mating, wing colour patterns may help provide camouflage for butterflies at rest (this is why the undersides are often so much less striking than the uppersides: see the illustrations of the Peacock and Small Tortoiseshell, for examples). They also in some cases distract predators from the vulnerable body of the butterfly. The vivid 'eye' markings of the peacock butterfly, on the outer tips of the wings, are a good example.

Adult butterflies have four wings, consisting, under the scales, of a thin, transparent membrane kept in shape by a framework of fine veins. These are usually visible even when covered with scales, and are useful points of reference when describing a butterfly's colour pattern or wing shape. Like most insects, the adult butterfly's body is divided into three distinct sections: head, thorax and abdomen. The butterfly's main sense organs are situated on the head. Most evident are the large rounded compound eyes. These are composed of thousands of tiny individual facets which combine to form an image of the surroundings. These give a rather poor impression of shape, but are sensitive to movement, and especially to colours: in fact, butterflies are believed to be sensitive to a wider range of wavelengths of light than any other group of animals. There are also simple eyes, or 'ocelli', which are believed to be sensitive mainly to light and shade. The two antennae are organs of chemical sense - taste and touch - and are used by females in finding the right plants for egg laying. They are also used to detect pheromones in courtship. Below and in front of the eyes is a pair of furry 'palpi', also organs of chemical sense. Finally, between them, and tightly curled up when not in use, is the unique 'proboscis', or tongue. This is a very long double tube which the butterfly can unfurl and use to probe deep into flowers to reach their nectar store.

The chest or 'thorax' is made up of three fused segments. To it are attached the wings and the (usually) six jointed legs. In flight, the wings perform a complex figure-of-eight pattern as they are flapped up and down. These actions are controlled indirectly by muscles which vary the shape of the hard outer 'skeleton' of the thorax. The abdomen is made up of ten joined segments. Along the sides, on each segment, are tiny breathing-holes, or 'spiracles', and enclosed within the final segment are the sexual organs.

AMAZING TRANSFORMATIONS: LIFE HISTORY

So far, we have described the adult butterfly only, but one of the most astonishing and fascinating aspects of the study of butterflies is their life histories. Each butterfly passes through four quite distinct stages during its life. First is the egg. This is tiny, and varies in shape according to the species concerned. Some, especially in the family of blue butterflies (Lycaenidae), have exquisite patterns of sculpturing over their surfaces that can only be seen under high magnification. In some species the butterfly over-winters in the egg stage, but more usually the egg hatches after about a week (sometimes hatching can be predicted by a change in colour of the egg), and a tiny caterpillar ('larva') emerges. Often the first meal of the caterpillar is its own eggshell.

The newly hatched caterpillar is totally unlike the butterfly it will (if lucky) eventually become. It is tubular in shape, with a distinct head at the front end. The head carries the mouthparts, generally adapted for chewing plant material, and small antennae and simple eyes. The rest of the body is usually quite soft and pliable, composed of 13 joined segments. There are six true legs, a pair on each of the first three segments, then, further back, several pairs of stubby 'pro-legs', and, finally, a pair of claspers at the rear end (in some moth caterpillars - the loopers - the pro-legs are absent). The caterpillar grows by periodically shedding its outer 'skin', in most species doing so four times before reaching its maximum size. The caterpillars of different species can usually be recognised by their distinctive shapes, colour patterns and by the hairs or, in some species, spiny projections, with which they are covered. This is complicated by the fact that in some species the colour pattern changes with the different stages (or 'instars') in the caterpillar's development. When full grown, the caterpillar becomes less active, and spins a pad of silk threads (in some groups, such as the skippers, they construct a cocoon, as do many moth species).

Clouded yellow caterpillar

After a resting period, the 'skin' splits for the last time to reveal a new stage in the

Clouded yellow Chrysalis

life history: the chrysalis, or 'pupa'. The shapes of some of the features of the adult butterfly (eyes, antennae, legs, the abdominal segments and miniature wings) are embossed on the surface of the chrysalis, but it has no means of movement from place to place, being confined to the occasional sideways wiggle of the abdomen. Though usually called a resting stage, within the chrysalis the most amazing changes are taking place. As the chrysalis stage progresses, groups of unspecialised cells located in different parts of the former caterpillar's body begin to develop as organs of the adult butterfly. Eventually, even the colour pattern of the future butterfly can be seen through the tough outer coating of the chrysalis. Finally, this outer coating splits down the back, and the butterfly emerges. At this stage its wings are crumpled flaps which are gradually 'pumped up' by blood being forced through the veins until they achieve their characteristic shape. Soon the wings harden, and the butterfly flits off to find its first drink of nourishing nectar.

HAZARDS OF BUTTERFLY LIFE

Beyond the female's careful selection of suitable places to lay her eggs, there is no parental care among the butterflies, and the vast majority of eggs laid never reach the adult stage. Many eggs are lost to animals that graze the plants on which they are laid, or die when grassland is cut. Caterpillars are eaten in great numbers by insectivorous birds. For example, a study carried out at the Institute of Terrestrial Ecology in England showed very high death rates of caterpillars and chrysalids of the White Admiral Butterfly caused by birds. Up to 80 per cent were lost from this single cause, but if the weather was warm the caterpillars developed more quickly and the birds were able to take fewer of them. Over-wintering at various stages in the life history is also a hazardous process, with risk of fungal and viral infections. In some species, again, there are huge losses to parasitic insects. These include parasitic wasps, especially those belonging to the family Ichneumonidae, and some groups of flies. These insects lay their eggs in the eggs or young caterpillars of their butterfly hosts. When these hatch, the resulting grubs feed on the soft internal tissues of their unfortunate victim, avoiding the destruction of vital organs until they themselves are fully grown. At this point they become pupae, either within the caterpillar's skin, or in groups around the dead body of their host. Sometimes, when butterflies are being bred in captivity, it can be a great disappointment to find that one's carefully tended caterpillars were parasitized in this way. However, the parasites themselves have fascinating life histories, and are well worthy of study in their own right.

So, with all these enemies, including ourselves, how do butterflies manage to survive at all? Parasites, of course, are dependent on leaving enough surviving members of the host species for their next generation to feed on: especially if they are specialised to attack only one species. It is now believed, for example, that the big fluctuations in numbers from year to year of the common blue butterfly of our urban gardens, the Holly Blue, are caused by its relationship to a specialised parasite. When the butterfly is common, the parasite finds its host easily and its numbers build up, so causing the butterfly to become more scarce. As this happens, the parasite, too, becomes more rare, and the butterfly population expands again. Caterpillars also have several means of defence from their enemies. Some are superbly camouflaged, with shape, colour and pattern often matching plant stems or the leaves on which they rest. The caterpillars of the Orange Tip and the Purple Emperor are excellent examples. Other caterpillars repel predators by their unpleasant taste, or by exuding nasty-smelling secretions. Some caterpillars, especially in the family of blues (Lycaenidae), secrete a sticky, sweet substance that is much appreciated by ants. Often the ants take the caterpillars down into their nests, where they gain food and protection from parasites. Yet another survival strategy is to feed together in large groups, giving the appearance of a single, much larger animal. Caterpillars of the Small Tortoiseshell, feeding on nettles, are a familiar example. Coordinated movements may also add to the protection by distracting a predator, and in some species the caterpillars tie protective sheaths of leaves around them with silk threads.

Even if the butterfly survives to the adult stage, it still faces many hazards. Long periods of bad weather prevent it from feeding or mating, but many species can find a sheltered spot deep among grass roots or up in the treetops. Here they remain inactive and conserve energy until better weather returns. A few species, such as the Small Tortoiseshell and Comma, pass the winter in this way, after building up their internal food stores in late summer and autumn. Apart from the weather, adult butterflies are attacked by predatory birds, small mammals and even frogs and toads. Other insects, too, present a threat: robber-flies, wasps and hornets and big hawker dragonflies can sometimes catch them as they fly. Especially sinister enemies of adult butterflies are spiders, notably *Misumena vatia*, a common crab spider which lies in wait on flower heads, pouncing on butterflies as they alight to sip nectar.

Adult butterflies lack 'offensive weapons' in the form of stings or bites, but as we saw above, the colour patterns on the wings are sometimes arranged so as to divert predatory attacks away from the vulnerable body of the insect. The sudden display of the very large and bright 'eye' markings on the wings of the Peacock butterfly has been known to startle a would-be predatory bird, allowing the butterfly to escape. The apparently haphazard flight of some species, with sudden, unpredictable changes of direction, probably also serves to outmanoeuvre and confuse predators. Other species, such as the adults of Nymphalids (including as the Red Admiral, Purple Emperor and Peacock butterflies) have powerful, rapid flight which enables them to evade capture on the wing. Finally, even very brightly coloured species often have cryptic undersides which match their surroundings when they are at rest.

Small tortoiseshell

BUTTERFLY BEHAVIOUR

The behaviour of adult butterflies varies from species to species and there is much that amateur butterfly watchers can do to add to our limited knowledge. Since butterflies are cold-blooded animals, their activity is largely controlled by their surrounding environment: especially by temperature and sunlight. Most species become inactive at night or in cool weather, but if alarmed some species will start a 'shivering' motion of the wings which raises the body temperature sufficiently for them to make a getaway

Common Blue

flight. Normally, however, they await the appearance of the sun to warm them up sufficiently for activity in the early morning or after a period of cool weather. To aid in this warming-up process, butterflies often stretch out their wings so as to expose the maximum surface directly to the sun's rays. The dark colours, especially, absorb the heat energy, and this is carried to the insect's body by the circulation of blood from the wing veins. I have observed a population of a Spanish species of blue butterflies move at sunset over the brow of a hillside from the east-facing to the west-facing slope so as to be in position to catch the early morning sun. Other species of blue butterflies which rarely open their wings in the heat of the day will do so in the very early morning after the chill of the night.

After warming up sufficiently, most butterflies are immediately off in search of food. This is usually gained from sipping nectar from flowers with the extended proboscis. Often this activity is aided by a sort of 'pumping' action achieved by repeated raising and lowering of the wings as the insect feeds. Some experiments have shown that butterflies react differently to various colours at different times of day, but it is unclear why this is so. Most butterflies will feed from a wide variety of flowers, and useful research can be done observing which species they visit, how far they fly to find suitable food sources, whether there is competition between members of the same species or between species for possession of choice nectar sources, and so on. In many species there are quite significant differences between males and females in the pattern of activity through the day. Males are often intensely involved in the pursuit of females, stopping only occasionally to feed at flowers. Females tend to be less active, feeding at flowers more persistently, and, after mating, intermittently indulging in spells of egg laying. However, there are many exceptions to this common pattern, and careful observation is worthwhile. In some species, notably the Purple Emperor and some blues, the insects will come down to feed on animal dung, or dead and rotting carcasses. Such species, together with some whites, are also often to be seen drinking at wet or damp patches of soil, or at the edges of streams ('mud-puddling'). It is often assumed that this behaviour is prompted by dehydration on hot days, but since it is mainly males which act in this way it seems likely that they are also taking in minerals important in the formation of sexually attracting scents ('pheromones'). Some of the species which hibernate as adult insects are often to be seen feeding from ripe or rotting fruit (blackberries, plums, pears and so on) in late summer and autumn prior to their long winter fast.

As with other aspects of behaviour, the reproductive activities of butterflies show many interesting variations from species to species. In some, the males fly considerable distances in their persistent search for females, often stopping to get a closer look (and, presumably, smell) at any appropriately coloured object which comes into their field of view. Males of the Large and Small Whites are familiar examples, as they fly close to the ground, investigating white flowers, scraps of white paper and so on, as they go. Commonly, species in which the males locate females in this way have widespread larval food plants and so are not closely tied to a particular territory. Other species (such as the Marsh Fritillary) have populations that are often limited to a small area where the caterpillars' food plants grow, and this area is treated as a kind of group territory. In yet other species the males establish an individual territory where they lurk, flying up only to confront intruding males or pursue passing females. Speckled Wood males are a good example of this, generally choosing perches in sun spots among shady woodland rides or lanes. Some species mark their territories with pheromones produced by glands on the male abdomen. The resulting scents may guide females to the male territory as well as signalling to other males that 'this territory is taken'.

When a male is lucky enough to approach a female his troubles may not be over. There is usually an initial courtship display (in some blues, for example, a rapid fluttering of the wings) during which pheromones are released from patches of scent scales on the male's wings. These scent scales ('androconia') are often gathered together to form visible black markings on the wings. These are most obvious in the males of some skipper butterflies and browns, but they are present in many others. If the female has already mated, she spreads her wings wide and raises her abdomen up towards the male. This posture looks quite provocative, and some observers mistake it for an invitation to the male. In fact it is a signal of rejection and the male eventually gives up trying to mate. When the female is freshly emerged and un-mated, she responds with a series of behavioural cues and the male moves round to her rear end and the pair mate back-to-back, attached at the tips of their abdomens. Sometimes the courtship sequence is very simple and rapid, but in other species it is complex and quite extended. In Wood Whites, for example, the pair face each other, and repeatedly 'doff' their antennae, flashing the white undersides to their tips. Subsequently their antennae are enclosed between the forewings of their partners, and they 'stroke' one another with extended probosces. In other species, courtship includes high, spiralling courtship flights. If the pair are not disturbed mating may last for some hours. If disturbed, they will fly off together, though only one of them (the male in some species, the female in others) will do the actual flying, simply carrying its mate along with it.

Egg-laying females generally go about this activity more or less hidden in vegetation. In some species, such as the Marbled White, the caterpillars feed on a variety of grasses and the females let their eggs drop freely among the food plants. More usually, however, the females carefully search out the correct food plant for the future caterpillars, and glue the eggs, one by one, or sometimes in large groups, on the plant tissue. Sometimes this may be on the underside of a leaf, sometimes at or close to a flower bud, or in the fork of a twig. Surprisingly, however, some species do not lay their eggs on the food plant at all, but in a carefully selected spot nearby. This is true of the Silver-washed Fritillaries, for example. The females lay their eggs singly in cracks in the bark of trees, as much as 4 to 5 m above ground level, leaving the newly hatched caterpillars to descend to the ground level to find the violet plants on which they feed. The caterpillars of most species are confined to feeding on just one, or a small number of closely related plants. This makes it particularly important that the females lay their eggs on or near a sufficient supply of the right plant species. They can often be observed carefully testing plants with their feet and antennae before finally settling on an appropriate plant to receive their

*Silver-washed
fritillary*

15

eggs. Whilst most caterpillars feed mainly on the leaves of their host plant, some burrow into the highly nutritious flower buds or seed pods.

One of the most surprising and little-understood aspects of butterfly behaviour is migration. The best-known global example is the trans-continental journeying of the American Milkweed butterfly, but several of our familiar European species also migrate. These include the Painted Lady, Large White and Clouded Yellow.

CLASSIFICATION

It is usual to group the European butterflies into eight families, of which two contain only one or two uncommon species. So, this guide concentrates on the remaining six families. Within each family there are sub-groupings of similar species, and if you want to identify a particular butterfly it is very useful to know which group it belongs to. This section is designed to help you do this:

1. **The swallowtails, apollos and festoons (Papilionidae):**
The members of this family are generally large- to medium-sized. The ground colour of the wings is usually whitish or pale yellow, with dark blotches, streaks or chessboard patterns:

   a. **Swallowtails:** have 'tails' projecting from the rear margin of the hindwings (pages 22-25).

   b. **Apollos:** have large dark blotches and often reddish spots. Wing margins quickly become semi-transparent (pages 26-27).

   c. **Festoons:** are similar to the swallowtails, but are smaller, and lack the 'tails' (pages 28-29).

2. **The whites, orange-tips and yellows (Pieridae):**

   a. **Whites:** medium-sized butterflies. The ground colour of the wings is white, often with black spots or marginal markings. The underside hindwings are often yellow or green and may be dappled green. They lack 'eye' markings on the underside hindwings - contrast with Marbled Whites (see below, pages 30-37 and 44-45).

   b. **Yellows:** all settle with wings closed. Some have black borders on the upperside (Clouded Yellows), but others have no black markings but projecting 'points' on the wing margins as with the Brimstone group. See pages 40-43.

   c. **Orange-tips:** like Dappled Whites, but with a patch of orange on the forewings, often only in the males (pages 38-39).

3. **The hairstreaks, coppers and blues (Lycaenidae):**

   a. **Hairstreaks:** are small butterflies that mostly settle with wings closed. The underside may be brown, greyish or green with a pale wavy or zigzag line. Look for the triangular outline of the butterfly on flowers (pages 46-55).

   b. **Coppers:** mostly small, bright, copper-coloured butterflies that shine in the sunlight. Some have a few small black markings, others are more strongly marked or suffused with black (pages 56-67).

   c. **Blues:** a very numerous group of small butterflies. In most species the males are blue on the upperside, but the females are often brown, or brown with a blue 'flush'. In a few species both sexes are brown (just to be confusing). Where the upperside is brown there is often a row of small orange spots along the wing margins. In most species the underside is pale greyish or fawn, with black spots, and often orange spots along the margins. The arrangement of the underside spots is often a useful guide to identification (pages 68-111).

4. The metalmarks (Riodinidae):
There is only one European species, the Duke of Burgundy. It looks like a small fritillary (see below and pages 112-113).

5. The nymphalids, fritillaries and browns (Nymphalidae):
This large and very diverse family is divided into two sub-families:

Brown Hairstreak

a. **The Nymphalinae: nymphalids (emperors, admirals and their allies) and the fritillaries:**

i. **Nymphalids:** medium to large butterflies that are powerful flyers, sometimes with contrasting black and white patterns, or brightly coloured with red, orange, and yellow with black markings. Includes several brightly coloured garden visitors (pages 114-133).

ii. **Fritillaries:** a very numerous group of medium- to large- sized butterflies. Almost all have orange-brown uppersides with a latticework of black marks. The markings on the underside hindwings are very variable and are essential for identification (pages 134-167).

b. **The Satyrinae: marbled whites, graylings, ringlets and browns:**
This is another very large and varied group, but contains some well-defined subgroups. The whole sub-family is distinctive in that the adults have only four fully developed legs (instead of the usual six):

i. **Marbled Whites:** white with black chessboard markings on the upperside. The undersides vary but usually have rows of 'eye' markings, in contrast to the whites, (see above, pages 168-169).

ii. **Graylings and their allies:** medium-sized butterflies that usually settle with wings closed. Broken grey or brown underside patterns camouflage them against rocks or tree trunks. Almost all have one or more prominent 'eye' markings close to the tips of the forewings (pages 170-189).

iii. **Ringlets:** a very numerous group (more than 40 European species) of similar species. Most have dark brown to blackish uppersides, often with red or orange bands containing variable numbers of 'eye' markings. Almost all live at moderate to high altitudes in mountains, but a few are found in the lowlands. This guide gives only a small selection of the more distinctive species. See pages 190-215.

iv. **Browns:** a varied group of mainly dark brown butterflies, usually with paler, orange patches on the wings, and small 'eye' markings close to the tips of the forewings (the Wall Brown looks similar to the fritillaries - see above). Others in this group (the heaths) are usually smaller and mainly orange-brown in colour. See pages 216-231.

6. The skippers (Hesperiidae):
These are small, fast-flying, moth-like butterflies that spend most of their time basking or perched on plants. Some are dark brown or grey-black with various paler markings (Grizzled and Mallow skippers) while others are mainly orange-brown. These have a distinctive way of posing with wings half open (see pages 232-251).

HABITATS AND CONSERVATION

Some butterflies can survive in a very wide range of habitats, but others have very specialised requirements (for example, the blue butterflies that depend on their association with a particular kind of ant). Throughout human history we have brought about great changes in our environment and these have affected the habitats of other living species. However, the changes that have occurred in Europe since the middle of the 20th century may have been more profound than any that went before. The great expansion of industry and urban dwellings has taken up much wildlife habitat, but at the same time the intensification and mechanisation of agriculture has transformed the remaining areas of countryside. The effects on butterfly populations have been drastic. The draining of wetlands has driven several species close to extinction. The intensification of lowland agriculture has affected many species, directly through the widespread use of chemical pesticides and indirectly by eliminating the wild grasses and flowers on which the butterflies depend. Woodland butterflies, too, have been badly affected by changes in woodland management: by the abandonment of coppicing, and in many areas by conversion of old, species-rich broad-leaved woodlands to monocultures of pine or *Eucalyptus*.

Luckily, some of the more remote parts of Europe, and the mountainous areas, have escaped these changes so far. Most of the mountain butterflies seem fairly safe, but the spread of intensive cultivation into new areas, especially in central and eastern Europe will destroy more butterfly habitat unless new policies are put into practice. In some countries there are laws against collecting some butterfly species, but often they are not seriously enforced. Even if they were, the main threat to butterflies is not collecting, but the destruction of the places where they live. Fortunately we do now have legislation both at EU and national levels to protect vulnerable habitats, and agricultural policy is shifting slowly in favour of more environmentally sensitive alternatives for the wider countryside. Still, these positive changes have not yet halted the decline towards extinction of many of our more specialised and vulnerable species. The main hope is that pressure from a concerned public will continue to make a difference. We now have well-supported and effective environmental organisations such as Butterfly Conservation in Britain and similar organisations in many European countries, some of them specialising in concern for butterflies (see page 256).

Finally, we often think of wildlife conservation as solely about protecting the countryside. However, the spread of urban living has not been wholly negative for butterflies. In fact, urban and suburban wasteland, roadside verges and railway cuttings, canal banks and ex-industrial sites often provide superb habitat for wildlife - including butterflies. This is partly because they have not been subjected to the intensive treatment of agricultural land. To these areas of towns and cities we can also add parks and gardens: together these add up to a huge green space. With the right, wildlife-friendly management these can compensate for the destruction of habitats that has gone on in the countryside. Perhaps most hopeful of all is that these urban wildlife havens become part of the everyday experience of the great majority of our human population: getting to know, appreciate and defend such places may be the best way to encourage a return of our declining butterflies.

GETTING CLOSE: HOW TO STUDY BUTTERFLIES

When, as a schoolboy, I began to appreciate butterflies, it seemed natural to make a collection of pinned specimens. The butterfly books of the time always had a chapter on catching, killing and setting our victims. I did make a small collection, but I never felt really happy about it, and I can remember being shocked at the long series of identical specimens in the cabinets of older collectors. In fact, of course, almost all of our current knowledge of butterflies has come from earlier generations of collectors, and there are scientific justifications for some collecting. However, for most of us this is not necessary. A modern SLR camera with a macro lens can capture the beautiful image of a butterfly on a flower without needing to harm it in any way. By showing details of behaviour, photography - even more so video photography - can add greatly to our understanding. Collecting butterfly eggs or caterpillars, breeding them through to adulthood, then releasing them in their habitats is another harmless way of studying them.

However, simply watching butterflies is both enjoyable and informative. Nowadays butterfly watching has become a popular activity, often as a result of birdwatchers switching to butterflies in the summer months. So much is unknown about the behaviour and habitat needs of even common butterflies, that amateurs can make many valuable discoveries. For example, if we need to argue for the protection of habitat we will have to provide evidence about the species present. Also, protected areas need to be managed correctly, and close monitoring of butterfly populations year by year is often required for this.

There is now a well-established way of monitoring butterfly populations. A route is chosen through butterfly habitats, and the observer walks this route regularly (say once a week through the season) at a standard speed. Notes can be made of all butterflies seen within a certain distance either side of the walk (for example, 3 or 5 m). An effort should be made to do the walk under similar weather conditions each time. If this is continued throughout the season, it gives good information about the flight periods of each species (their phenology), and also about their different habitat preferences. If it is continued over a period of years, then it gives good evidence of fluctuations in the populations of each species. For those of us with too many constraints on their time to do such systematic counting, there is still much to learn from direct observation of individual butterflies. They can be watched through binoculars without any disturbance to their activity. Sketches and written notes can be made of significant observations. Increasingly, butterfly watchers make use of tape recorders, the camera and video recorders.

PHOTOGRAPHING BUTTERFLIES

This is a challenging and frustrating - but also very satisfying - hobby. Each butterfly photographer has to find her or his particular approach, so there is no 'right' method. The basic equipment is a single lens reflex camera (film or digital) and a macro lens (preferably one that gives a maximum ratio of the object to image of 2:1, or, better, 1:1). This should enable you to almost fill the frame with an image of even the smallest of European butterflies. When choosing a lens it is also advisable to find one that allows you to focus in on your quarry from as far away as possible. The closer you have to get, the more likely you are to frighten off the butterfly. A flat-field 2x converter

Geranium Argus

fixed between the camera and macro lens will help with this, and a good one will not lead to noticeable deterioration in the quality of your pictures. However, with this set-up you will almost certainly need to mount one or two flash units on the camera, as natural light will not give enough illumination. Trial and error will be needed to get as natural a look as possible, but the problem of darkened or black backgrounds is difficult to solve. Some photographers prefer to take their chances with natural light, and often use a telephoto lens.

But the equipment is only a small part of what is needed. It is best to start with common, local butterflies - with your own garden, if you have one. You will need to observe their behaviour and for each species take note of when it settles and when it is most easily approached. In the middle of hot, sunny days most species are very active and difficult to approach. Usually the best times are early morning, late afternoon, or when the sun re-emerges after a cool and overcast spell. When taking nectar from flowers or basking in early or late sunshine butterflies are often quite easy to approach. This is particularly true if they are fond of compound flowers with numerous florets on a single head, where they are often preoccupied for some considerable time.

A note on how to approach a butterfly: they are often more sensitive to movement than to shape. This means that you should avoid all sudden movements, and approach them as slowly as is consistent with getting focussed on them before they fly off. An alternative is to wait close to an attractive nectar source until the butterfly comes to you. Some butterflies are very sensitive to sound, and most will also be alarmed if you cast a shadow over them.

It is important not to be too depressed if your first results are disappointing. You learn with practice, but you should always expect to throw away (or delete) the majority of photos you take. Once the hobby takes hold, you may find yourself planning holidays to remote places where you have a chance of finding some rare or localised butterfly, and, if you have a tolerant family, this could be the beginning of a lifetime of enjoyment. I have spent more than 25 years seeking out the butterflies of Europe, and have still not managed to find quite all of them. However, I have had some wonderful trips, visited special, remote and awesome places, and enjoyed the companionship of fellow butterfly watchers from all parts of the continent.

TECHNICAL TERMS

Wherever possible, the use of technical terms and jargon have been kept to a minimum throughout the book, and in many instances less familiar terms have been explained in the context
where they have been used. Nevertheless, the study of butterflies necessarily involves some
words and phrases that require further explanation, a few of which are defined here.
Words in italics are defined elsewhere in the glossary.

Abdomen: the rear section of the butterfly's body, composed of ten connected segments. It contains the reproductive organs, a large part of the digestive system, and has air holes (spiracles) at the sides of each segment for breathing.

Androconium (plural, Androconia): specialized scales, often concentrated in dark bands on the wings of male butterflies. They have gland cells that emit *pheromones* during courtship.

Antenna (plural, Antennae): the long filamentous feelers attached to the butterfly's head between its large, compound eyes. They are sensitive to touch, but are especially important as organs of chemical sense (taste and scent).

Coppicing: a traditional practice of woodland management. Trees valuable for mature timber were left as standard trees, with an understorey of trees or shrubs such as hazel or small-leaved lime that were cut back every few years to provide smaller wood products for such purposes as fencing, charcoal burning and tool making. The open woodland structure encouraged the growth of wild flowers on the woodland floor and benefited butterflies and other wildlife. The system has been restored in many woodlands as part of conservation management.

Flight period: the period of time during the season when the adult butterflies can be seen. Some species may have more than one flight period in a year.

Generation: butterflies mate and the females lay their eggs during the *flight period* of the adults. If the resulting caterpillars take a full year to reach the adult stage and start their life cycle over again, this is said to constitute a single generation in a year. Some species can complete their life cycle more quickly, and have two or more *flight periods* in a year, and so two or more generations.

Habitat: a general term used to characterize the typical living conditions in which a species thrives. This includes the other animals and plants with which it is associated, as well as aspects of the physical and chemical environment, climatic conditions and so on (for example deciduous woodland, upland moors, subalpine meadows).

Larva (plural, Larvae): the early, growing stage in the life history of an insect. In most species the larvae are grub like, with a simplified external structure. As they grow, they shed

their 'skin' several times before entering the resting (*pupal*) stage, before finally emerging as an adult insect. In some insects (such as dragonflies) the early appearance is more similar to the adult form, and they are referred to as nymphs. These insects lack the ***pupal*** stage. The *larvae* and *pupae* of butterflies are referred to as caterpillars and chrysalids respectively.

Ocellus (plural, Ocelli): small, simple eyes, with only a single lens. Most insects have three of them on the top of the head, but adult butterflies have just two. Most visual sensation is received through the large, compound eyes.

Palpi: these appear as small furry pads on the front of a butterfly's face, surrounding the *proboscis* when it is not in use and coiled up. Under the fur they are small, jointed projections from the head, and act as organs of scent and taste.

Parasite: an organism that obtains all or most of its nutritional needs from another, either by invading body tissue, or attaching itself to the outer covering. Parasites vary in the amount of harm they cause to their hosts, but generally avoid killing them.

Phenology: the study of the timing of the various events and processes in the lives of organisms, for example the timing of the *flight periods*, or emergence from hibernation. Concern with climate change has stimulated much interest in this topic recently.

Pheromone: a complex chemical compound that is released into the environment and is used in scent communication between animals, including butterflies.

Proboscis: the long double tube that butterflies use to suck up nectar from flowers, or other fluids from damp earth or decaying organic matter. When not in use it is coiled up under the head.

Pupa (plural, Pupae): the resting stage between the *larval* growing stage and the final emergence of the adult insect. While in the pupal stage an astonishing reorganization of the internal organs takes place, and the structures of the future adult form within the outer casing of the pupa. In butterflies and moths the pupa is often referred to as the chrysalis.

Thorax: the middle part of the butterfly's body, between the head and the *abdomen*. It contains part of the digestive and respiratory system, and also carries the legs and two pairs of wings.

Swallowtail

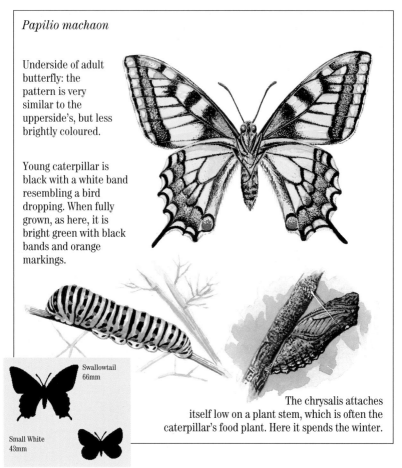

Papilio machaon

Underside of adult butterfly: the pattern is very similar to the upperside's, but less brightly coloured.

Young caterpillar is black with a white band resembling a bird dropping. When fully grown, as here, it is bright green with black bands and orange markings.

Swallowtail
66mm

Small White
43mm

The chrysalis attaches itself low on a plant stem, which is often the caterpillar's food plant. Here it spends the winter.

One of the most strikingly beautiful of the European butterflies, the Swallowtail occurs throughout the continent in a wide variety of habitats, from lowland meadows and marshes to dry hillsides and mountain slopes. It is often seen over hill-tops and cliff-edges, soaring majestically on air currents. Swallowtails sip nectar from a wide variety of flowers, but are especially attracted to thistles, and will often visit garden flowers. In Britain and parts of northern Europe they are limited to wetland or coastal habitats, where they can be seen flying powerfully over reed beds, only occasionally stopping to bask in the sun, or take nectar from a flower. Eggs are laid singly on the leaves of fennel, wild carrot or other members of the umbel family. In Britain and southern Scandinavia they use milk parsley almost exclusively.

Sipping nectar from valerian. They bask and take nectar with open wings, displaying the distinctive yellow and black pattern, with blue scaling and red spots towards the rear of the hindwings. The yellow ground colour is variable, sometimes almost white.

WHERE Throughout Europe, except the far north. Very localized in south-eastern England.

WHEN In England and parts of northern Europe adults fly in May and June, with a partial second brood in July and August. In much of southern Europe they can be seen all through spring and summer months.

LOOKALIKES

There are three other European swallowtails. **The Corsican Swallowtail** (*Papilio hospiton*) is very similar, but is confined to the islands of Corsica and Sardinia. The **Scarce Swallowtail** (page 24) and **Southern Swallowtail** (*P. alexanor*) are more distinctive.

Scarce Swallowtail

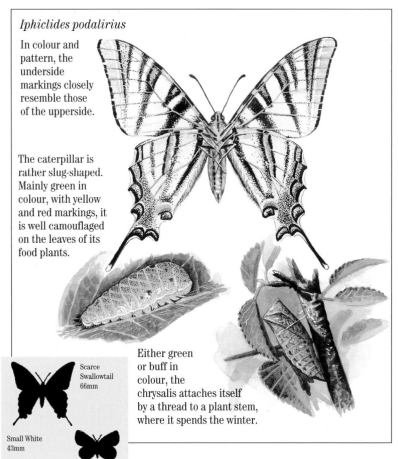

Iphiclides podalirius

In colour and pattern, the underside markings closely resemble those of the upperside.

The caterpillar is rather slug-shaped. Mainly green in colour, with yellow and red markings, it is well camouflaged on the leaves of its food plants.

Scarce Swallowtail 66mm

Small White 43mm

Either green or buff in colour, the chrysalis attaches itself by a thread to a plant stem, where it spends the winter.

Common and widespread throughout most of Europe, the Scarce Swallowtail's long, tapering black stripes, and long tails to the hind-wings are highly distinctive. The ground colour varies from pale yellow to whitish, with males usually paler than females. A large form with a paler ground colour that occurs in south-western France and Spain is sometimes considered to be a distinct species. Adults lay their eggs on a wide variety of cultivated and wild trees and shrubs, especially blackthorn, cherry and other *Prunus* species, and apple and hawthorn.

They are often seen in suburban gardens and parks as well as in open countryside, where they feed from flowers such as thyme and lavender. Their flight can be swift and powerful. While basking with wings spread open, or visiting a flower, they are easily approached.

The upperside of the Scarce Swallowtail. Note the long black streaks across the pale background, the rather pointed forewing shape, and the long 'tails' on the hindwings. These are quickly damaged, and older specimens often lack one or both.

WHERE Throughout Europe, except Britain, Scandinavia, Holland and Denmark. Occasional migrant specimens are seen in these countries.

WHEN Depending on latitude and altitude, it can complete up to three generations a season. In the south it can be seen from March to October.

LOOKALIKES

Black markings on the forewings form stripes, rather than blocks as in the **Common** (page 22) and **Corsican** (*Papilio hospiton*) swallowtails. In the **Southern Swallowtail** (*P. alexanor*) black bands in the middle of the forewings end abruptly.

Apollo

Parnassius apollo

Upperside of the adult. Note the variable orange to red spots on the hindwings.

The caterpillar has short hairs. It is mainly black, with bright orange markings along its sides, and small blue 'warts' along the back. It feeds only in direct sunlight.

The chrysalis is formed in a loose cocoon concealed beneath a rock or among mosses or leaf litter. Reddish-brown, but with a blue-grey dusting on the surface.

Apollo
70mm

Small White
43mm

This fine butterfly has many named colour variations, and this may be one reason why it has attracted butterfly collectors – so much so that it is a legally protected species in most places. The butterfly has a slow, flapping flight and spends much of its time drinking nectar from flowers of the thistle family. After mating, the male secretes a structure known as the sphragis, which is attached to the abdomen of the female and prevents her from mating again. The eggs are laid on plant stems or on evergreen shrubs, and the winter is usually spent as a larva still within the eggshell. The caterpillars feed on the succulent leaves of plants in the stonecrop family. The favoured haunts of the butterfly are mountain slopes and meadows, often on limestone, with rocky outcrops and crags, but at lower altitudes in Scandinavia.

Apollo shows its underside as it feeds from a knapweed flower head. Note the translucent wings. The white-centred red rings on the hindwing are quite variable, sometimes orange or yellowish.

WHERE Throughout the European Alps, and in other mountainous areas including the Massif Central in France and the Pyrenees. In southern Scandinavia it tends to favour coastal districts.

WHEN One generation in a year, and the adult butterflies are most frequently seen in June and July.

LOOKALIKES

The **Small Apollo** (*Parnassius phoebus*) is very similar, but usually has less grey shading, especially on the hindwings. It is confined to the Alps. The **Clouded Apollo** (*P. mnemosyne*) is smaller and lacks red markings.

Spanish Festoon/Southern Festoon

Spanish Festoon
Zerynthia rumina

Southern Festoon
Zerynthia polyxena

Caterpillar of Spanish Festoon. Both species' caterpillars are fawn to dark grey, with brush-like projections along their backs and sides.

Undersides of adult *rumina* and *polyxena*. The underside markings of both species closely resemble the uppsersides.

Spanish Festoon/ Southern Festoon 42-46 mm

Small White 43mm

Chrysalis of Spanish Festoon. When fully grown, the caterpillar wanders away from the food plant and then becomes a chrysalis, which is attached by fine threads to a rock or firm plant stem. The chrysalis is fawn in colour, with darker grey markings. It spends the winter in this stage.

Both these butterflies look like small Swallowtails - except they lack the 'tails' on the hind wings. The **Spanish Festoon** has several well-marked red spots on the forewing, but these are much reduced or absent in the **Southern Festoon.** The females of both species lay their eggs singly or in small batches on the leaves of various species of birthwort (*Aristolochia*). Like their larval food plants, they inhabit dry rocky hill-sides, gullies, dry riverbeds and scrubby meadows They spend the night settled with wings closed on dead flower heads, with their abdomen curved below in a very characteristic posture. Much of their time is spent resting with open wings exposed to the sun. Males occupy distinct ter-ritories and soon return to their favoured basking spot after being dis-turbed. In Provence you may see them flying together.

Upperside of Spanish Festoon. *There are several red spots on the forewing, and the black marginal 'zigzag' is not so acutely angled as in the Southern Festoon.*

Upperside of Southern Festoon. *The forewing has red spots only near the apex of the forewing, or none. Note the shape of the black 'zigzag' near the wing margins.*

WHERE AND WHEN Southern France; widespread in Spain. Flies in spring, mostly from April to June. In warm places and seasons they also produce later broods. In southern Spain it can be seen right through the winter

Spanish Festoon

Southern Festoon

WHERE AND WHEN Further east than Spanish Festoon; in Italy, eastern Europe and the Balkans. Also flies in spring, most commonly April to June. In warm places and seasons, it too may produce later broods.

Black-veined White

Aporia crataegi

Upperside of male Black-veined White. Note the white wings, unmarked except for black (dark brown in the female) outlining of the veins. The scales are thinly distributed on the wings, giving a slightly translucent appearance.

The fully grown caterpillar has short hairs, and has a black band along its back, bordered by two orange-red bands. It feeds on the leaves of both wild and cultivated fruit trees.

Black-veined White 58mm

Small White 43mm

The chrysalis is pale yellowish or greenish, with black markings, and is usually formed close to the ground, often on a blade of grass.

This butterfly occurs in a variety of habitats including hedgerows, roadsides, woodland glades, gardens and orchards. Females lay their eggs in large batches on the undersides of leaves of shrubs and trees in the rose family, especially blackthorn and cultivated fruit trees. As well as visiting flowers for nectar, the adults sometimes gather in large numbers to drink fluid from damp soil. Caterpillars feed collectively in their early stages, and are seen as a pest of fruit orchards in some parts of Europe. This was true in England during the 19th century, but the butterfly was extinct here by the mid 1920s. Young caterpillars hibernate together, and begin feeding on the fresh shoots in spring. Adults frequently stop to feed from flowers such as clovers, cranesbills and thistles. They often roost collectively, as shown in the photograph.

A collective roost of Black-veined Whites on valerian in a woodland glade. This butterfly can be very abundant in favourable habitats. They roost with wings closed, but often bask in sunshine with wings spread.

WHERE The Black-veined White is common and widespread throughout Europe except for Britain and northern Scandinavia.

WHEN The flight period depends on latitude, but is usually from May until July.

LOOKALIKES

No other European species has white wings, unmarked except for dark outlining of the veins.

Large White

Pieris brassicae

Male upperside: brilliant white on the upperside, with a black tip to the forewings.

Female upperside of Small White. Note the more creamy-white ground colour, and less intense black markings.

The caterpillar is green with a yellow line down its back, and black mottling. It is subject to the parasitic activity of a wasp whose larvae feed inside the caterpillar until fully grown, and then form yellow cocoons around its dead body.

Large White 55mm

Small White 43mm

The chrysalis is attached by a silken thread and pad to a solid surface, often on a wall or under a window frame. It is pale green with small yellow and black markings, and the insect spends the winter in this stage.

The underside hindwings are pale greenish or greyish in colour with a dusting of grey scales in the spring brood, but often yellowish in the summer. The black markings tend to be more intense and contrasting in the later broods. The adult butterflies are not territorial and they fly considerable distances, the males in search of females, the females seeking out suitable plants on which to lay their eggs. Once they have found a place, they lay their eggs in batches of 50 or more and the resulting caterpillars feed in groups, stripping the leaves of their food plants. They choose members of the cabbage family, often cultivated ones such as cabbages and Brussels sprouts. They inhabit allotments and suburban gardens as well as the farmed countryside, but are often difficult to approach for photography. The species is threatened by the increased use of pesticides.

A female of the first brood feeds from a dandelion. The black markings are more intense in the later summer broods. They usually close their wings when drinking nectar from a flower, but they bask with open wings early and late in the day.

WHERE Found throughout Europe, though at high altitudes and in the extreme north it is mainly represented by migrant individuals: some are known to fly tens of kilometres.

WHEN In southern Europe they can be seen from March to October, but in the north they are restricted to two broods, in spring and mid-summer.

LOOKALIKES

The **Small White** (*Pieris rapae*) is very similar, but smaller, and the black markings are less intense, especially in spring broods. The **Southern Small White** (*P. mannii*) and the **Mountain Small White** (*P. ergane*) are confined to southern Europe and are quite localised.

Green-veined White

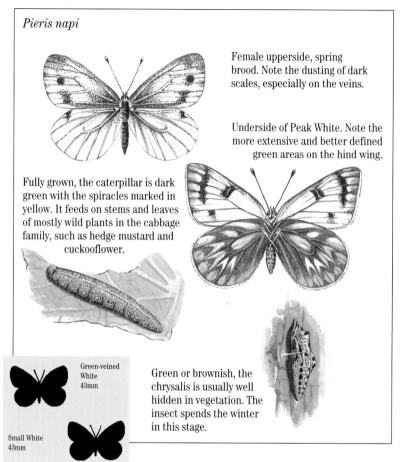

Pieris napi

Female upperside, spring brood. Note the dusting of dark scales, especially on the veins.

Underside of Peak White. Note the more extensive and better defined green areas on the hind wing.

Fully grown, the caterpillar is dark green with the spiracles marked in yellow. It feeds on stems and leaves of mostly wild plants in the cabbage family, such as hedge mustard and cuckooflower.

Green-veined White
43mm

Small White
43mm

Green or brownish, the chrysalis is usually well hidden in vegetation. The insect spends the winter in this stage.

Superficially, this species could be mistaken for the Small White, but the beautiful greenish outlining of the veins of the yellow underside hindwing marks it out. The males of the spring brood are brilliantly white on the upperside, with a darkened tip to the forewing and often a black central spot. In later broods and in southern Europe the green veining on the underside is less well marked. As the caterpillars' food plants tend to grow in damp meadows, ditches or stream banks and marshy field corners, that is where the butterfly is most likely to be seen, often flying together with the Orange-tip. The adults are not strictly territorial, but they are less mobile than either the Small or Large White. Like other whites they bask in the sun early and late in the day. They are more easily approached than are the Large and Small whites.

Underside of a male, spring brood. Males are more often seen in spring basking with open wings, while the females visit flowers or seek out plants on which to lay their eggs. The beautiful yellow underside ground colour is less apparent in later broods.

WHERE Throughout Europe, to the extreme north of Scandinavia. It remains common, but has suffered from drainage associated with intensification of agriculture.

WHEN Three or even four generations in a season in most parts of Europe: adults are seen from March or April through to August or September.

LOOKALIKES

In mountains and some northern areas there are forms of *Pieris napi* sometimes treated as distinct species, with yellow not white ground colour. The **Peak White** (*Pontia callidice*) has a lattice of green lines on the underside, and flies in the Alps and Pyrenees.

Bath White

Pontia daplidice

Upperside of female Bath White. Note the extensive black markings.

Underside of Dappled White. Compare the pattern of green markings on the hindwing with that on the Bath White, opposite.

The fully grown caterpillar is violet-blue, with yellow lines along the body, and tiny black raised points. It feeds mainly on the flowers and developing seeds of its food plants, and is vulnerable to parasitic wasps.

The greyish chrysalis has tiny black markings, and is suspended by a girdle of silk, usually to the stem or seed head of the food plant.

Bath White
40mm

Small White
43mm

Some authors divide up the eastern and western European populations of this butterfly into two species, but they are identical in appearance. In both sexes the black markings on the forewings are more extensive than those of the other common white butterflies, and the regular pattern of green scaling on the underside hindwings is distinctive. The males have fewer black markings on the upperside, and very little or no black round the edges of the hindwings. The adult butterflies can fly fast and direct, often staying close to the ground. They favour dry, open areas, particularly fallow fields, arable margins and recently disturbed 'brownfield' sites, where the caterpillar's food plants grow. These are most frequently flowers in the mignonette group, pepperworts, hedge mustard, shepherd's cress and other weeds that readily colonize such habitats.

A female settles to feed. Note the even olive green of the dark pattern on the underside and around the forewing tip. Just visible is the upperside forewing tip, with its black and white pattern, and thin white line through the black mark close to the leading edge.

WHERE Common and very widespread as far north as the southern tip of Scandinavia. Not a regular breeder anywhere in Britain, seen there only as a rare migrant.

WHEN Several generations a year; in southern Europe adults seen from March to October. In northern Europe, they appear later in the year.

LOOKALIKES

The green mottling on the underside distinguishes this species from all except the **Orange-tip** (page 38) and the **Dappled Whites**. There are several of the latter in southern Europe, and the green markings on the underside are more irregular.

Orange-tip/Moroccan Orange-tip

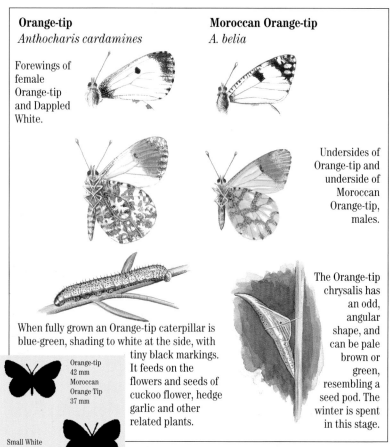

Orange-tip
Anthocharis cardamines

Moroccan Orange-tip
A. belia

Forewings of female Orange-tip and Dappled White.

Undersides of Orange-tip and underside of Moroccan Orange-tip, males.

When fully grown an Orange-tip caterpillar is blue-green, shading to white at the side, with tiny black markings. It feeds on the flowers and seeds of cuckoo flower, hedge garlic and other related plants.

The Orange-tip chrysalis has an odd, angular shape, and can be pale brown or green, resembling a seed pod. The winter is spent in this stage.

Orange-tip 42 mm
Moroccan Orange Tip 37 mm

Small White 43mm

The distinctive orange-and-white pattern on the upperside of the male **Orange-tip** is distinctive, but females lack this, and are often mistaken for Small Whites. However, the underside hindwings in both sexes are distinctive: irregularly mottled yellow or green, dusted with darker scaling. This is a butterfly of damp meadows, ditches and hedgerows, where the main food plants of its caterpillars grow. They establish set routes, usually close to stands of the caterpillar's food plants, which they patrol regularly in search of females. Females leave a scent when laying their eggs singly on flower heads, warning off subsequent visitors: the caterpillars are cannibalistic. The **Moroccan Orange-tip** is similar, but the ground colour of the male upperside is yellow, and there is less green on the underside hindwings. The eggs are laid on flower heads of buckler mustard.

Male Orange-tip. *This male Orange-tip takes a brief break from patrolling for females to drink nectar from cuckooflower, one of the food plants of the caterpillar. The pattern of white ground colour and orange patches is unique.*

Male upperside of Moroccan Orange-tip. *The male has a beautiful sulphur-yellow upperside, with orange patches on the outer part of the forewing. The female lacks the orange patches, but has a narrow rust-brown arc around the wing-tips.*

WHERE AND WHEN Orange-tip is very widespread all over Europe, including Scandinavia. Seen from late March or early April through into June, or later at higher altitudes.

Orange-tip

Moroccan Orange-tip

WHERE AND WHEN Moroccan Orange-tip is confined, in Europe, to the south. It flies from March to July, depending on locality.

Clouded Yellow

Colias crocea

Upperside of male (above) and upperside of female (below). The brilliant orange-yellow with black borders distinguishes them from all other common species. Note the yellow spots in the black borders of the female.

The caterpillar is green with a yellow line along each side, and orange rings round the spiracles. It feeds on plants in the pea family. Where resident, it spends the winter in this stage.

Attached to the food plant, the chrysalis is mainly pale green, with some yellow markings.

Clouded Yellow 47mm

Small White 43mm

The males of this species fly powerfully and tirelessly low over open ground in search of females, stopping occasionally to take nectar from a flower. The black borders in the female are broken by a row of yellow spots, and the ground colour of her wings is sometimes (form *helice*) pale grey-white. Cultivated land where legumes are still grown as part of crop rotation can attract huge numbers of Clouded Yellows. However, as it is a strongly migratory species, individuals can be seen almost anywhere, including uncultivated land near coasts. They are able to complete two or three generations in a season and numbers build up through the summer and autumn. Like other members of the Clouded Yellow group, they always roost and rest with their wings closed. When taking nectar from a flower they are fairly easy to approach for photography.

Underside of a male Clouded Yellow. As they always settle with their wings closed it can be difficult to be sure which species you are seeing. Here, the unbroken dark border to the forewing shows through, confirming this is a male.

WHERE Throughout Europe, in open ground, cultivated or uncultivated, often near coasts in Britain and Scandinavia.

WHEN In the south of Europe adults fly all year round, but migrate throughout Europe during the spring and summer. As far north as Britain they rarely arrive before May.

LOOKALIKES

The most widespread look-alikes are the **Pale** (*Colias hyale*) and **Berger's Clouded Yellows** (*C. alfacariensis*). These species are almost indistinguishable from each other, but differ from the Clouded Yellow in having a much paler ground colour to the wings.

Brimstone

Gonepteryx rhamni

Upperside of male Brimstone: clear sulphur-yellow wings, with distinctive points on the margins. The females are much paler, greenish-white on the upperside, and pale green to whitish on the underside (see lookalikes).

Upperside of male Cleopatra. Note the orange patch, and slightly different wing shape (see lookalikes).

The caterpillar is blue-green with a pale stripe along each side. It feeds on the leaves of buckthorn or alder buckthorn, and is perfectly camouflaged as it rests along the mid-rib of a buckthorn leaf.

Brimstone
55mm

The chrysalis is green, with an angular shape, well camouflaged among low vegetation.

Small White
43mm

These are among the small number of butterflies that hibernate as adults, and they are one of the first species to be seen in early spring, when they can be seen feeding from sallow catkins and other spring flowers. In spring, the females lay their eggs singly on fresh leaves of young buckthorn trees. In summer, the offspring of these butterflies can sometimes be seen in large numbers in the woodland rides or lanes where the buckthorns are common. They soon disperse, and the males can be seen flying across open countryside, often well away from known breeding sites. They feed actively from thistles, teasel, bramble and other flowers to build up their reserves for the winter. They often hibernate in evergreen shrubs, especially ivy, where they are very well camouflaged. They always settle with their wings closed.

A female Brimstone feeds from bramble before hibernating. Both sexes feed actively in summer and early autumn, and are more easily approached than in the spring. Note the prominent points on both fore- and hindwings.

WHERE Widely distributed in woods and hedgerows throughout Europe, except for northern Scandinavia.

WHEN After hibernation some individuals survive until early July, after their offspring have emerged. These continue to fly through August; sometimes well into autumn. Among the longest-lived butterflies.

LOOKALIKES

The **Cleopatra** (*Gonepteryx cleopatra*) is very similar, but has a bright orange patch on each forewing in the male. Females are more difficult to distinguish, but the wing shape is more rounded, and the points less prominent in the Cleopatra.

Wood White

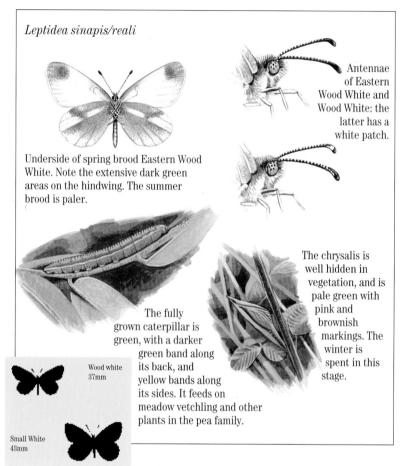

Leptidea sinapis/reali

Antennae of Eastern Wood White and Wood White: the latter has a white patch.

Underside of spring brood Eastern Wood White. Note the extensive dark green areas on the hindwing. The summer brood is paler.

The fully grown caterpillar is green, with a darker green band along its back, and yellow bands along its sides. It feeds on meadow vetchling and other plants in the pea family.

The chrysalis is well hidden in vegetation, and is pale green with pink and brownish markings. The winter is spent in this stage.

Wood white 37mm

Small White 43mm

This rather frail-looking butterfly is the smallest of the common 'whites'. The uppersides are plain white, apart from a dark patch at the tip of the forewing. This is less clearly defined and sometimes almost absent in the female, and her wing shape is more rounded. The underside hindwing in both sexes is greenish white, with ill-defined bands of darker scaling. The males have a weak, fluttering flight, but are seemingly tireless as they fly along woodland rides in search of females. The females are more often seen taking nectar from a variety of woodland-edge flowers or laying their eggs on their caterpillar's food plants. The courtship is unique, with the male facing the female, tongue stretched out, and 'flashing' the white spots on the underside of the tip of his antennae. They sometimes gather to sip fluid from damp patches on rides, and always settle with wings closed.

A male Wood White feeds from a flower of herb Robert in a woodland ride. The white underside of the tip of the antenna shows quite clearly, and the dark patch at the apex of the forewing shows through faintly on the underside. The female's wing is more rounded.

WHERE Throughout Europe, including much of Scandinavia, but very localized in the north. Has declined markedly in Britain, and is vulnerable to the shading out of its habitats.

WHEN In southern Europe up to three generations a year, and can be seen from early spring to September. In Scandinavia a single summer brood.

LOOKALIKES

The **Eastern Wood White** (*Leptidea duponcheli*) is found in southern Europe. It differs from the Wood White in having much more densely dark-scaled underside hindwings in the spring brood, and also lacks the white patches on the undersides of the antennae.

Brown Hairstreak

Thecla betulae

The eggs are very conspicuous, and often the best way of discovering the presence of this elusive butterfly.

The male upperside is uniformly dark brown except for small orange marks at the rear of the hindwings, and a variable pale area at the centre of the forewing.

When ready to pupate, the caterpillar drops to the ground and forms the dark brown chrysalis. It is sometimes buried in a loose cell by ants.

The fully grown caterpillar is slug-shaped, and green in colour with yellow stripes. It suspends itself from the underside of a leaf during the day and starts to feed at dusk.

Brown Hairstreak 35mm

Common Blue 28 mm

The dominant colour of the female upperside is a deep brown, but with wide orange patches or bands on the forewings. Although quite widespread, this butterfly is not often seen. The adults spend much of their time congregating high up around 'master trees' in hedgerows or woodland edges, where they feed on honeydew left by aphids. The females are more frequently seen as they come down to take nectar from flowers such as bramble and hemp agrimony, as well as to lay eggs. The plants chosen for this are blackthorn shrubs, and it is usually the lower branches that are used, the dumpy white eggs being placed singly in the fork of a twig. Unusually for hairstreaks, the butterflies often bask with their wings open during sunny periods, but they can remain motionless for long periods of poor weather. The winter is spent as an egg.

A Brown Hairstreak drinks aphid honeydew from a bramble leaf. Note the two thin white 'hairstreaks' across the hindwing, and the short 'tails' projecting from the margin. They are often easy to see when basking in sunshine, but they disappear in dull weather.

WHERE Along woodland edges and on farmland where there remain dense networks of hedges managed in a traditional way. Throughout Europe, including southern Britain and Scandinavia.

WHEN One generation a year, with adults emerging mid-July onwards and flying until early October.

LOOKALIKES

No other European species has an orange-brown underside with double 'hairstreaks'.

Purple Hairstreak

Favonius (Quercusia) quercus

Undersides of Purple Hairstreak: silver-grey, with a white stripe across both fore- and hindwing, and a black-centred orange spot near the edge of the hindwing. As in most hairstreaks, there is a short 'tail' on the hindwing.

The upperside of the male Purple Hairstreak is very dark, almost black, with a purple sheen covering most of the wing surface.

Underside of Spanish Purple Hairstreak (see lookalikes). Note the absence of the 'hairstreak'.

The caterpillar is brown with darker diagonal markings along its sides. It lives in a silken shelter by day and feeds on oak leaves at night.

Purple Hairstreak 34mm

Common Blue 28mm

The chrysalis is formed on the ground beneath an oak tree and is often tended by ants.

These butterflies spend most of their time settled or flying around the tops of oak trees, and can be observed through binoculars. Sometimes they come down to lay eggs on twigs or leaf buds on lower branches, or take nectar from thistle or bramble flowers. In early morning they open their wings and bask for a while. Most often we see only the underside as they probe flowers for nectar, or lick ant honeydew from leaves. Like many other insect species, the purple hairstreak has a close association with oak trees. The butterflies form huge colonies with as many as hundreds of thousands of individuals in large oak woods, but they will also live on oaks in hedgerows and even isolated old oak trees in parkland. The females lay their tiny greyish eggs on or near flower-buds on oak twigs, and the caterpillars do not hatch until the following spring.

A female Purple Hairstreak basks on an oak leaf in early morning. The purple patches catch the light from certain angles and change in intensity as the butterfly moves.

WHERE In oak woods, or around hedgerows and isolated oak trees throughout Europe as far north as southern Scandinavia.

WHEN Depending on locality, the butterflies may be seen from late June to early September, but numbers usually peak in July.

LOOKALIKES

The **Spanish Purple Hairstreak** (*Laeosopis roboris*) occurs in Spain and the south of France. It lacks the white streak across the underside.

White-letter Hairstreak

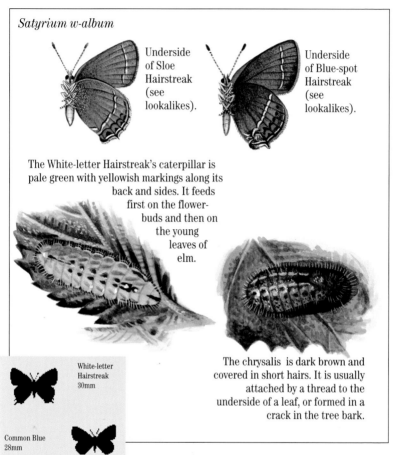

Satyrium w-album

Underside of Sloe Hairstreak (see lookalikes).

Underside of Blue-spot Hairstreak (see lookalikes).

The White-letter Hairstreak's caterpillar is pale green with yellowish markings along its back and sides. It feeds first on the flower-buds and then on the young leaves of elm.

White-letter Hairstreak 30mm

Common Blue 28mm

The chrysalis is dark brown and covered in short hairs. It is usually attached by a thread to the underside of a leaf, or formed in a crack in the tree bark.

Like the Purple Hairstreak, the White-letter spends much of its time in the treetops, and sometimes several can be seen flying in and out of the canopy of an elm tree. They feed from honeydew secreted by aphids, but occasionally come down in numbers to sip nectar from nearby thistles or bramble blossom. When they do so they can be picked out by looking for the characteristic triangular outline of the underside, with the w-shaped white 'hairstreak' from which it derives its name. The butterflies never open their wings except to fly. The epidemic of Dutch Elm Disease destroyed many trees, and with them the colonies of White-letter Hairstreaks that lived on them. However, the butterflies were able to survive on the regrowth of the trees from suckers, and populations have recovered in some parts of Europe, including Britain.

A White-letter Hairstreak feeding from a bramble flower. Note the clear white 'w' shape on the hindwing, the orange band near the margin, and the small, projecting 'tails'. When drinking they appear sleepy, and are easy to approach for photography.

WHERE Woods and hedgerows with surviving elm trees throughout Europe, except northern Scandinavia and northern Britain.

WHEN Usually on the wing from mid-June through July.

LOOKALIKES

Ilex, (*Satyrium ilicis*) **False Ilex**, (*S. esculi*) **Sloe** (*S. acaciae*) and **Blue-spot** (*S. spini*) hairstreaks are similar, but the white streak does not form a distinct 'w'; the Blue-spot Hairstreak has a blue spot on the hindwing. Also **Black Hairstreak** (page 52).

Black Hairstreak

Satyrium pruni

The fully grown caterpillar is pale green with thin yellow lines on its sides, and tiny reddish-purple warts along its back. It feeds on buds and young leaves of blackthorn.

Upperside of female Black Hairstreak

The chrysalis is black with white markings, resembling a bird dropping. It is usually attached by a thread to a twig.

Black Hairstreak 32mm

Common Blue 28mm

This is a woodland butterfly that, like other members of its group, spends much time up in the tree canopy. The butterflies feed on aphid honeydew, and often rest on exposed leaves with their bodies angled side-on to the sun. They make occasional darting flights out of the foliage and along an open ride, only to disappear again. They occasionally come down to take nectar from bramble, privet or dogwood blossom, or to lay their eggs. For this they require mature stands of blackthorn, and the eggs are generally laid singly on young twigs 1.5 m. or more above the ground. They are threatened by changes in woodland management and also by suppression of regrowth of the blackthorn by grazing deer. The winter is spent in the egg stage, and the newly-hatched caterpillar feeds on flower-buds in early spring.

A male Black Hairstreak perches on a leaf with closed wings. Note the white 'hairstreak' running across both hind- and forewings. This does not quite form the clear 'w' shape of the White-letter Hairstreak, and the orange band is much more prominent in this species. Look for the butterflies on privet blossom in woodland rides.

WHERE Along the edges of mature woodland or old hedgerows, but sparsely distributed in most of Europe. In Britain it only occurs in the East Midlands, and in Scandinavia only in the south.

WHEN The butterfly has a relatively short flight period, usually from mid-June to mid-July.

LOOKALIKES

This species differs from the **White-letter Hairstreak** (page 50) and the others in this group in having a much wider orange band and a row of black spots on the underside.

Green Hairstreak

Callophrys rubi

Upperside of a male Green Hairstreak

Underside of a Chapman's Green Hairstreak (see lookalikes).

The fully grown Green Hairstreak caterpillar is yellowish green with a narrow green line along each side and pairs of yellow spots along its back.

Underside of Provence Hairstreak (see lookalikes).

The Green Hairstreak chrysalis is dark brown with short hairs, and is formed among leaf litter on the ground. It can emit an audible squeak and is often attended by ants. Winter is spent in this stage.

Green Hairstreak 32mm

Common Blue 28mm

The Green Hairstreak is usually found in the vicinity of shrubs, which are the most common food plants of its caterpillars. On heathland, gorse and broom are commonly used, but the caterpillars will also feed on dogwood, bramble and buckthorn. On chalk downland the butterfly lays its eggs on bird's-foot trefoil and rock-rose, and on moorland bilberry is used. The butterflies are superbly camouflaged when at rest on the leaves or branches of shrubs. The male occupies a perch from which he makes regular flights over and around nearby bushes in search of females. If he encounters another male a prolonged twirling 'dance' is performed until the winner returns to his perch. They lay their eggs singly on or near flower buds, and these form the food of the caterpillar. When at rest the adult butterflies do not open their wings.

A Green Hairstreak at rest. Like most other hairstreaks they always rest with closed wings, showing only their undersides. The pattern of bright green with a dotted white line across the wings is quite unique. The line of white spots is often reduced and occasionally absent.

WHERE Widespread and often common in shrubby habitats throughout Europe

WHEN A spring butterfly, emerging from the chrysalis in March or April, and flying through to early June.

LOOKALIKES

Chapman's Green Hairstreak (*Callophrys avis*) has brown rather than white borders to the eyes. **Provence Hairstreak** (*Tomares ballus*) has green underside hindwings, but orange forewings with black spots. Both are scarce and confined to southern Europe.

Small Copper

Lycaena phlaeas

Underside of Small Copper. Note the lack of a strongly marked orange band on the hindwing.

Male upperside of Violet Copper; note the blue sheen (see lookalikes).

The caterpillar is green, often with pink along its sides. It feeds on the underside of the leaves of its food plant.

The chrysalis is formed among leaf litter on the ground, and is pale brown in colour with darker specks.

Small Copper
28mm

Common Blue
28 mm

This butterfly is one of the smallest of the 'copper' group, and is also the most common. In both sexes the ground colour of the forewings is a bright copper, with black spots and a black border. The hindwings are black with a copper border. Some specimens have a row of bright blue spots on the hindwing. They live in a variety of dry, open habitats, such as heathland, old grazing meadows, roadside verges and recently disturbed brownfield sites. They favour places with sparse vegetation, and patches of bare soil or stones. Here males sunbathe with open wings and periodically fly out in search of females, or to chase off an intruding butterfly. The females lay their eggs singly on the upperside of leaves of sorrel or sheep's sorrel. The winter is spent as a small caterpillar. They occur in small numbers.

A female Small Copper basks in the sun. Its preference for dry, sparsely vegetated habitats and its small size distinguish it from the Large Copper, while the contrasting pattern of the hindwing and dark border to the forewings separate it from other coppers.

WHERE In suitable habitats throughout Europe, including the far north.

WHEN The butterfly can complete several generations in a year, three or more in southern Europe, two in the north. The adults can be seen from early spring through to October or even November.

LOOKALIKES

The **Violet Copper** (*Lycaena helle*) male has a blue sheen on the upperside, while the female has blue spots on the forewings. It is very local in wetlands. Females of other coppers are often similar, but have more strongly marked undersides.

Large Copper

Lycaena dispar

The distinctive upperside of the male is copper-coloured and marked only by the narrow black border and a small black spot at the centre of each forewing.

The underside of the female large copper is strongly marked and silver-grey.

The caterpillar is pale green with darker markings on the back and along the sides. It feeds on the underside of dock leaves, and spends the winter when part grown.

The chrysalis is pale brown with darker brown and white markings, and is attached by a pad and silk girdle to a stem of the food plant.

Large Copper
28mm

Common Blue
28mm

This is the largest of the 'copper' group. The female resembles a large version of the small copper, but her strongly marked silver-grey underside is distinctive. The northern form is larger and brighter, but now only occurs in The Netherlands. A similar form occurred in the fens of eastern England, but became extinct in the mid-19th Century. This form lays its eggs on water dock only, and is now known to require an abundance of this plant, spread over a large area. The remaining fragments of fenland in Britain proved too small to maintain a viable population. The more widespread European form is generally smaller, and lives in a wider range of damp flowery grasslands. It is becoming increasingly scarce as its habitats are destroyed by modern farming practices. Males patrol territories and mark them with scent, often at some distance from their food plants.

A female Dutch form of the Large Copper drinks from a dandelion. This large, bright form is rare; the more usual form, rutilus, *has the same basic pattern. The copper marginal band on the hindwing extends into the rest of the wing. Occasionally seen too in Small Copper.*

WHERE Widespread, but very localised throughout Europe, but absent from Scandinavia and Britain.

WHEN The northern form flies in July and August, but in central and southern Europe it has two flight-periods: May-June, and July-August.

LOOKALIKES

The male **Scarce Copper** (page 60) is similar on the upperside, but the white spots on the underside are distinctive in that species.

Scarce Copper

Lycaena virgaureae

Upperside of the female: an orange ground colour, with dark spots that merge on the hindwing.

Underside (both sexes are similar). The line of white spots separates this from all other species.

The fully grown caterpillar is green with paler markings along the sides and back. The winter is spent in the egg stage, or as a small caterpillar.

Scarce Copper 32mm

Common Blue 28mm

The chrysalis is pale greenish or fawn, with black mottling, and is usually attached to a leaf of the food plant.

The brilliant, copper-coloured upperside of the male is unmarked except for the narrow black border, and row of small black spots. When settled with their wings open, the colours of both sexes shimmer in the sunlight. The butterfly inhabits flowery meadows and open woodland, from lowlands to more than 2,000 m in altitude. Much of its time is spent taking nectar from a wide range of flowers, including scabious, thistles and yellow flowers in the dandelion family. While in this mode it makes only short flights between flowers. In the middle of the day both sexes often rest in tall vegetation with wings open to the sun. The females lay their eggs on the leaves of several plants in the dock family – often common sorrel. At high altitudes, the females are darker, and in the Pyrenees the males often have a few small black spots on the forewings.

A male Scarce Copper rests on a flower-head. Notice the unmarked, shimmering copper-colouring of both fore- and hindwings. The fine black border of the hindwings is extended inwards to form semi-detached spots, while the black border on the forewings gets gradually wider around the wing tip.

WHERE The butterfly is widespread in Europe, but absent from north-west France, Britain and northern Scandinavia.

WHEN Only one generation in a year. The adults can be seen from late June through July and August, depending on altitude.

LOOKALIKES

The male **Large Copper** (page 58) is similar but has black spots in the middle of its forewings, and lacks the underside white spots.

Sooty Copper

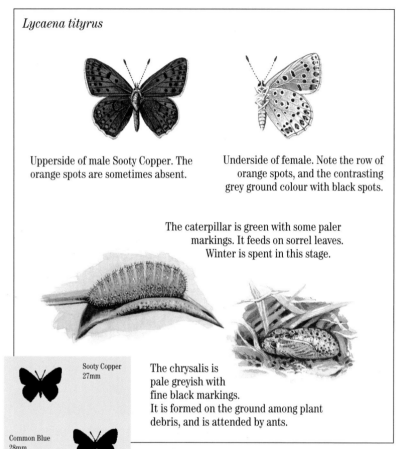

Lycaena tityrus

Upperside of male Sooty Copper. The orange spots are sometimes absent.

Underside of female. Note the row of orange spots, and the contrasting grey ground colour with black spots.

The caterpillar is green with some paler markings. It feeds on sorrel leaves. Winter is spent in this stage.

The chrysalis is pale greyish with fine black markings. It is formed on the ground among plant debris, and is attended by ants.

Sooty Copper
27mm

Common Blue
28mm

The Sooty Copper is well named, as the male upperside is very dark brown, sometimes with a few orange markings close to the wing borders. Its forewings are more pointed than those of other coppers, and the hindwings are sharply angled at the rear. The butterflies are often found in hot, sheltered and flowery places, where they bask with open wings or sip nectar from a wide range of flowers such as clovers, ox-eye daisies, fleabane, thyme and mints. At higher altitudes, the males often lack orange markings. In mountainous areas the females, too, have much less orange on their wings, and may have completely dark brown uppersides. The females lay their eggs singly on the leaves of plants in the dock family, especially sorrels. They fly swiftly but rarely fly far, and can usually be approached for photography.

A female Sooty Copper basks between bouts of egg laying. In this specimen the dusky brown ground colour of the hindwings is suffused over part of the forewings. The amount of orange colour varies, and some individuals resemble the Small Copper. But note the lack of a wide, dark forewing border.

WHERE Widespread and often common throughout Europe, but absent from Britain and almost all of Scandinavia.

WHEN In warmer areas, adults may be seen from April through to October, but in cooler climates and at higher altitudes it has two generations: May-June and July-August.

LOOKALIKES

The male could be confused with the female of the **Purple-shot Copper**, (page 64) but size and wing shape should be enough to distinguish them.

Purple-shot Copper

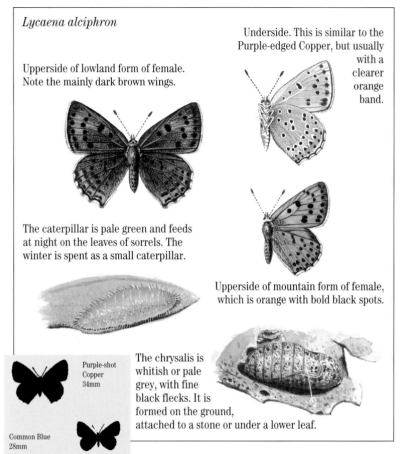

Lycaena alciphron

Upperside of lowland form of female. Note the mainly dark brown wings.

Underside. This is similar to the Purple-edged Copper, but usually with a clearer orange band.

The caterpillar is pale green and feeds at night on the leaves of sorrels. The winter is spent as a small caterpillar.

Upperside of mountain form of female, which is orange with bold black spots.

Purple-shot Copper 34mm

The chrysalis is whitish or pale grey, with fine black flecks. It is formed on the ground, attached to a stone or under a lower leaf.

Common Blue 28mm

The male has copper as the ground colour of the upperside with black spots and a narrow black border, but what marks it out is the purple sheen overlying the copper. This shimmers in sunlight and gives the butterfly a uniquely beautiful appearance. The amount of purple varies between individuals, and is much reduced in populations at high altitudes and also in the south of Europe. The typical females are mainly dark brown and quite different from their brightly marked sisters of the *gordius* form. The butterflies fly in flowery meadows, often in the company of other coppers, where they spend much of their time taking nectar from ox-eye daisies, thyme, mint, marjoram and other flowers. Eggs are laid singly on the leaves of sorrels. The males often rest with their wings open, when they are easily approached for photography.

A male Purple-shot Copper rests on a flower head of ox-eye daisy in a lowland meadow. The pose with half open wings is typical. Note the purple suffusion, most clearly visible on the forewings. In southern and upland forms the purple colouring is limited to the wing margins or absent.

WHERE Widespread in Europe, but more common in the south and east. Absent from Britain and Scandinavia.

WHEN In most areas there is just one generation in a year, and the adults are most often seen from mid-June through July and into August. In southern France they fly as early as April.

LOOKALIKES

See **Sooty Copper** (page 62). Males of the high altitude form could be confused with the **Purple-edged Copper** (page 66), but have more black spots on the upperside.

Purple-edged Copper

Lycaena hippothoe

Upperside of typical female: orange forewings with black markings and mainly black hindwings with an orange border.

The underside is similar to that of the Purple-shot Copper, but usually with a reduced orange band on the hindwing.

The caterpillar is green with ill-defined paler markings, and usually feeds on sorrels and other plants in the dock family.

The chrysalis is off-white, with black spots and stripes, and is formed close to the ground.

Purple-edged Copper 33mm

Common Blue 28mm

The upperside of the male is deep copper-coloured, with a black central spot in each forewing, and a dark suffusion on the inner half of the hindwing. The purple reflection on the leading edge of the forewings and on the hindwings is variable, and may be absent at high altitudes. The butterflies inhabit boggy areas and wet grassland in lowland areas, but also fly in subalpine meadows up to 2,500 metres. The high altitude forms of the female lack the orange colouration and are mainly dark brown on the upperside. The eggs are laid singly on leaves or stems of sorrels or docks. Purple-edged Coppers bask with their wings open in early morning and late afternoon, often with many of them close together, and can easily be approached for photography. The winter is spent as a small caterpillar.

A male Purple-edged Copper basks in sunshine after a spell of cool weather. In this specimen the black spot in the middle of the forewing is faint, but still visible. Note the purple reflections along the leading edge of the forewings and across part of the hindwings.

WHERE In suitable habitats throughout Europe, but absent from north-west France and Britain.

WHEN In northern and western Europe, one generation in a year, flying from June to early August (later at high altitudes).

LOOKALIKES

The females could be confused with those of several other copper females, but can usually be distinguished by the undersides.

Long-tailed Blue

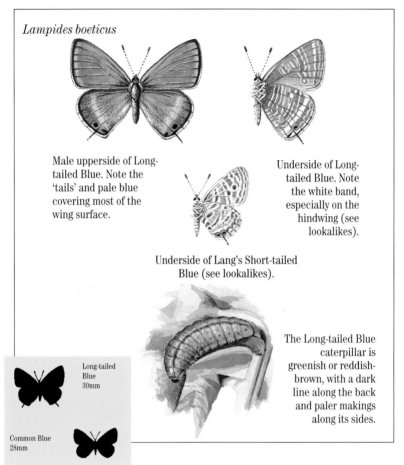

Lampides boeticus

Male upperside of Long-tailed Blue. Note the 'tails' and pale blue covering most of the wing surface.

Underside of Long-tailed Blue. Note the white band, especially on the hindwing (see lookalikes).

Underside of Lang's Short-tailed Blue (see lookalikes).

Long-tailed Blue 30mm

Common Blue 28mm

The Long-tailed Blue caterpillar is greenish or reddish-brown, with a dark line along the back and paler makings along its sides.

Adult Long-tailed Blues are often seen taking nectar from bramble or thistle flowers, or, sometimes, sipping fluid from damp patches on the ground. When they do so, they usually keep their wings closed, showing the white underside with fawn-coloured striations, and, on the hindwing, two dark spots close to the 'tails'. Both sexes bask in full sunshine with open wings: plain blue, shading to dark grey at the edges in the males, and dark grey with a blue flush in females. The male adopts a perch on a high branch of a bush, from which he flies out to search for females or chase off other males. The females lay their eggs on many species of plants in the pea family, especially bladder senna, brooms, and everlasting sweet pea. The caterpillars feed inside the pods on developing seeds.

A female Long-tailed Blue sips nectar from bramble blossom. The extent of the blue flush at the base of the wings varies. In older specimens one or more of the tails may be lost, but the black spots on the rear of the hindwings are distinctive.

WHERE Widespread and often common in warm, flowery habitats with shrubs, migrating through Europe from its Mediterranean strongholds. Rarely seen in Britain or Scandinavia.

WHEN Flies all year in the far south of Europe, but from May to October further north.

LOOKALIKES

Lang's Short-tailed Blue (*Leptotes pirithous*) is very similar in appearance and habits, but the underside striations are evenly distributed. There is a white band on the underside of the Long-tailed Blue.

Geranium bronze

Cacyreus marshalli

Upperside of female. Note the chequered white wing margins.

The caterpillar is pale green with red markings when fully grown. Seen here on a Pelargonium leaf.

Geranium Bronze
22-25mm

Common Blue
28 mm

This butterfly is a native of southern Africa, and was introduced into Mallorca by accident, probably as a caterpillar on imported plants. It soon spread to be a pest on cultivated *Pelargonium* species, and from its first recorded presence in 1990 has spread rapidly in southern Europe. It often rests on dry twigs or dead leaves with its wings closed. When it does so, the whitish underside, with its irregular grey-brown markings, gives astonishingly good camouflage. It sometimes rests with its wings half open, revealing the plain dark brown upperside. This has one or more black spots near the 'tail' at the rear of the hindwing, and distinctive chequered white margins. Males are smaller than the females, otherwise the two sexes look identical. In southern Europe they may have adapted to wild species of *Geranium*.

A Geranium Bronze shows its underside markings as it drinks nectar from a flower. The irregular pattern of white-bordered grey-brown blotches and bands is unique. The butterfly rarely opens its wings while feeding, but will do so when at rest on sunny days.

WHERE Parks and gardens with the food plant as well as dry scrubland in southern Europe. It is still uncommon further north, but seems to be spreading.

WHEN Adults can be seen at any time of year in Mediterranean Europe.

LOOKALIKES

The irregular pattern on the underside of the wings as described above is unique to this species.

Short-tailed Blue

Cupido (Everes) argiades

Upperside of female Short-tailed Blue. The blue 'flushes' are variable and sometimes absent.

Underside of Short-tailed Blue. Note the two orange spots on the hindwing.

Underside of Provençal Short-tailed Blue, lacking orange markings (see lookalikes).

The caterpillar is green with whitish hairs, but becomes red-brown prior to hibernation.

Short-tailed Blue 28mm

Common Blue 28mm

The chrysalis is pale green or brownish-yellow with black markings. It is usually attached to the underside of a leaf.

The upperside of the male is plain blue, often tinged with violet, and with a narrow black border, while the female is brown with a blue flush at the base of the wings. In later broods the blue on the female is often reduced to just a scattering of scales. The 'tails' on the hindwings are not obvious, and are sometimes lost in older specimens. The butterfly is found in sheltered, flowery meadows and scrubland, often in quite small areas and close to water. They fly fast, but usually only for short distances. When basking with wings part-open they are not difficult to approach. The caterpillars feed on the flowers and developing seeds of various species of plants in the pea family, especially clovers, trefoils, crown vetch and bird's-foot trefoils. The winter is spent in the egg stage in the north, but as a fully grown caterpillar in southern Europe.

A male Short-tailed Blue basks on water mint. A narrow black border to the wings gives way to a marginal row of tiny black spots on the hindwing. Otherwise the plain blue upperside is unmarked. Tiny 'tails' project from the rear of the hindwings.

WHERE Widespread in southern and central Europe, but becoming scarce northwards. Absent from Britain and Scandinavia.

WHEN Flies in three generations from April to October in the south, but is reduced to two flight periods (May/June and July/August) in the northern part of its range.

LOOKALIKES

The **Provençal Short-tailed Blue** (*Cupido alcetas*) lacks the orange spots on the underside hindwing. The **Little Blue** (page 74) and **Osiris Blue** (*Cupido osiris*) lack the 'tail' on the hindwing.

Little Blue

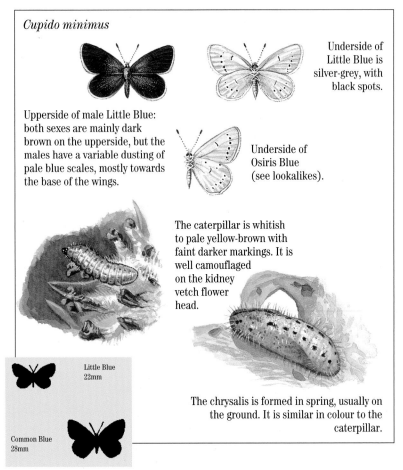

Cupido minimus

Underside of Little Blue is silver-grey, with black spots.

Upperside of male Little Blue: both sexes are mainly dark brown on the upperside, but the males have a variable dusting of pale blue scales, mostly towards the base of the wings.

Underside of Osiris Blue (see lookalikes).

The caterpillar is whitish to pale yellow-brown with faint darker markings. It is well camouflaged on the kidney vetch flower head.

Little Blue
22mm

Common Blue
28mm

The chrysalis is formed in spring, usually on the ground. It is similar in colour to the caterpillar.

The Little Blue is one of the smallest of all European butterflies, and easily overlooked. They are found in sheltered hollows and grassy areas among shrubs, often occupying quite small areas of suitable habitat. They can fly very quickly and soon disappear from view when disturbed. In most parts of Europe the caterpillar's food plant is kidney vetch, although several species of milk vetch (*Astragalus*) are also reported, and the butterflies form small colonies where the food plant grows. The kidney vetch flourishes on chalk or limestone grassland, and colonizes areas of bare ground on sand dunes, quarries or road cuttings. The males establish favourite perches on the tips of vegetation, and tend to remain in the same small area. The fertile females lay their eggs in the flower heads of the kidney vetch, and the resulting caterpillars feed on the developing seeds and surrounding tissues.

A female basks on horseshoe vetch. The species' small size and unmarked, dark brown uppersides with prominent white wing fringes separates it from most others. However, female Short-tailed Blues that have lost their tails can look very similar.

WHERE The butterfly is widespread throughout Europe, but is more local and generally coastal in Scandinavia, and scarce in northern England.

WHEN Often a single prolonged flight period from May to July, but in some areas there are two generations, flying in April to June and again from August to September.

LOOKALIKES

The female of the **Osiris Blue** (*Cupido osiris*) is very similar, but the row of black spots on the underside forewing tends to be straight, as opposed to curved in the little blue. The male Osiris Blue is bright blue on the upperside.

Holly Blue

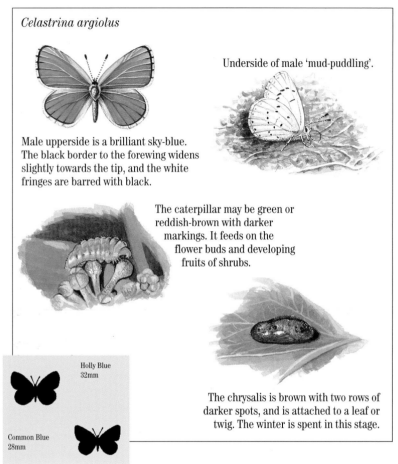

Celastrina argiolus

Underside of male 'mud-puddling'.

Male upperside is a brilliant sky-blue. The black border to the forewing widens slightly towards the tip, and the white fringes are barred with black.

The caterpillar may be green or reddish-brown with darker markings. It feeds on the flower buds and developing fruits of shrubs.

The chrysalis is brown with two rows of darker spots, and is attached to a leaf or twig. The winter is spent in this stage.

Holly Blue
32mm

Common Blue
28mm

This is a familiar butterfly of woods, gardens and scrubland. The female has much wider black borders to her wings than the male. Both sexes have pale powder-blue undersides, with tiny black spots. They bask on exposed leaves or twigs early in the morning, but the males soon turn to searching for females. They 'contour' bushes and hedges for long periods, stopping only occasionally to rest with wings open to the sun or to drink nectar from flowers, especially bramble. They can often be seen drinking fluids from damp soil or mud patches. The females are more often seen at rest or laying their eggs on flower buds of the caterpillars' food plants: often holly in spring, and ivy in late summer, but a wide range of other shrubs is also used. Numbers fluctuate greatly from one year to the next as a result of parasite attacks.

A female Holly Blue basks in early morning sunshine. Often habitat alone will help to identify this butterfly, as it flies close to the trees and shrubs on which it lays its eggs. Note the distinctive wide, black forewing borders. This is more extensive in second-brood females.

WHERE Absent from northern Britain and scarce in northern Scandinavia, but otherwise common and widely distributed throughout Europe.

WHEN There are two generations each year, in April and May, then in July and August.

LOOKALIKES

The pale sky-blue underside, with black spots and no orange is unlike any other European butterfly.

Green-underside Blue

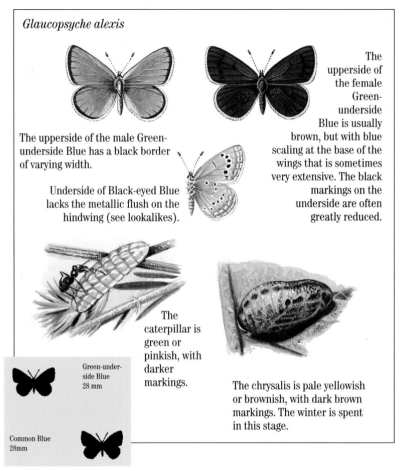

Glaucopsyche alexis

The upperside of the female Green-underside Blue is usually brown, but with blue scaling at the base of the wings that is sometimes very extensive. The black markings on the underside are often greatly reduced.

The upperside of the male Green-underside Blue has a black border of varying width.

Underside of Black-eyed Blue lacks the metallic flush on the hindwing (see lookalikes).

The caterpillar is green or pinkish, with darker markings.

The chrysalis is pale yellowish or brownish, with dark brown markings. The winter is spent in this stage.

Green-underside Blue 28 mm

Common Blue 28mm

The extensive green/ blue metallic flush on the underside hindwings is distinctive of this species. The butterfly inhabits sheltered woodland clearings or open areas in scrubland. The eggs are laid on the flower buds of many species in the pea family, especially sainfoins, milk vetches, and crown vetch. The resulting caterpillars feed on the flowers and developing seeds. Like many other species in the blue family, the caterpillars are attended by ants. These are attracted to sugary secretions from the caterpillar, and are believed to protect it from parasites. In dull weather and at night the adults roost, often many specimens together, on tall grass stems. They roost with their heads facing down and wings closed, and are surprisingly well-camouflaged.

A Green-underside Blue drinks nectar from sainfoin. Note the blue-green metallic flush on the basal part of the hindwing, with a row of small black spots, and a row of large spots on the forewing.

WHERE Widespread in southern and central Europe and southern Scandinavia, but absent from Britain and much of northern Europe.

WHEN One generation in a year, and the adults fly from April through to early July.

LOOKALIKES

The **Black-eyed Blue** (*Glaucopsyche melanops*) is similar but smaller, and lacks the metallic flush on the underside. It has a row of faint pale marginal markings on the forewing.

Large Blue

Maculinea arion

The underside of the Large Blue is pale brown with black spots and a greenish metallic flush around the base of the hindwing.

Underside of Alcon Blue lacking the metallic flush (see lookalikes).

Large Blue
40 mm

A red ant adopts a Large Blue caterpillar.

The chrysalis is pale yellowish-brown, and is formed inside the ants' nest.

Common Blue
28 mm

The Large Blue belongs to a small group of European species all of which are dependent on ants to complete their life history, and are threatened by habitat changes wherever they still occur. The oval black spots and black central spot on the forewing are distinctive. The dark grey borders are wider in the female, and are still wider at high altitudes. The eggs are laid on the flower buds of thyme or marjoram, and the young caterpillars begin feeding on the flowers and developing seeds. Soon, however, they drop to the ground and secrete a sugar solution that attracts ants. The caterpillar is carried into the ants' nest and is fed by them. It is now known that the caterpillar only thrives in the nests of one species of red ant. The butterfly was at one time extinct in Britain, but has since been successfully reintroduced.

A male Large Blue perches with open wings. The wide black border and arc of black spots around a central mark on the forewing is distinctive. At high altitudes the dark border is more extensive.

WHERE Widespread, but often scarce, in central and southern Europe, southern Scandinavia and (following reintroduction) southwest England.

WHEN The butterfly has one generation in a year and can be seen in June and July.

LOOKALIKES

The **Scarce Large Blue** (*Maculinea telejus*) has a silvery-blue upperside, and the **Dusky Large Blue** (*M. nausithous*) has a dark brown underside. The **Alcon Blue** (*M. alcon*) lacks the metallic flush on the underside hindwing.

Baton Blue

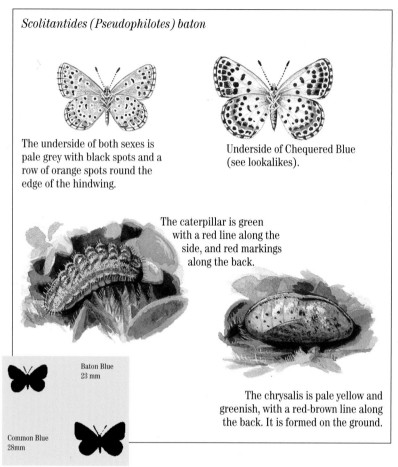

Scolitantides (Pseudophilotes) baton

The underside of both sexes is pale grey with black spots and a row of orange spots round the edge of the hindwing.

Underside of Chequered Blue (see lookalikes).

The caterpillar is green with a red line along the side, and red markings along the back.

Baton Blue
23 mm

Common Blue
28mm

The chrysalis is pale yellow and greenish, with a red-brown line along the back. It is formed on the ground.

Males have bright, silvery-blue uppersides, with a black border. The white fringes of the wings are laddered with black. The upperside of the female is dark brown with variable amounts of pale blue scaling. A close relative of the Baton Blue is widespread in eastern Europe. Though usually treated as a seperate species, it is identical in colour-pattern, and can only be distinguished by minute anatomical features. Baton Blues live in sheltered and sunny habitats with abundant thyme. The eggs are laid on the flower buds of thyme, or sometimes other plants in the deadnettle family such as various mints and lavenders. The caterpillars feed on the flowers and developing seeds and they are attended by ants. The butterfly spends much of its time basking with open wings, and often drinking from damp soil.

A male Baton Blue basks in the sun. Its upperside is bright, silvery-blue with a black spot in the middle of each wing, and prominent black-and-white laddered wing fringes. It is the most widespread of a small group of very similar butterflies.

WHERE Southern and western Europe; absent from Scandinavia and Britain.

WHEN At low altitudes there are two flight periods: April to June, and again in July to September. At higher altitudes there is just one summer brood.

LOOKALIKES

The **Chequered Blue** (*Scolitantides orion*) is much more local and southern. The black underside markings are much more prominent. Several other related species fly in south-western and south-eastern Europe.

Silver-studded Blue

Plebejus argus

The male underside is greyish or whitish with black spots and a row of orange spots around the wing margins. On the hindwings there is typically a shiny metallic spot next to each orange one, though sometimes some or all of these are replaced by black.

Male upperside of Idas Blue (see lookalikes).

The caterpillar is green with a dark band along the back and paler markings on its sides.

The chrysalis is pale brown and usually formed inside an ants' nest.

Silver-studded Blue 25 mm

Common Blue 28mm

This small, jewel-like butterfly is abundant in some localities, but loss of its habitat has led to the extinction of many local populations, especially in the northern part of its European range. The violet-blue males are more noticeable than the females, which are brown on the upperside, with a variable row of orange spots around the wing margins. The female underside is like that of the male, but has a brownish ground-colour. The butterflies live in a variety of habitats: lowland heaths, chalk or limestone downs and vegetated sand dunes. Winters are spent in the egg stage, and the resulting caterpillars feed during the spring on heathers or gorse on heathland, or a range of small plants in the pea family on calcareous grassland.The caterpillar secretes a sugary liquid, which attracts black ants. These protect the caterpillar and chrysalids from parasites.

A male Silver-studded Blue basks with open wings. This little butterfly is very variable, but the upperside is usually distinguished by the wide dark border, and fine black outlining of the outer portion of the wing veins. The ground colour usually has a violet tint.

WHERE Throughout Europe, but scarce in northern Scandinavia and extinct in northern Britain.

WHEN In the northern part of its range there is one flight period, through July and August, but further south it completes two generations in a year.

LOOKALIKES

The **Idas Blue** (*Plebejus idas*) is very similar, but usually has narrower black borders on the upperside. However, both species are very variable and close examination is needed to identify them with certainty.

Geranium Argus

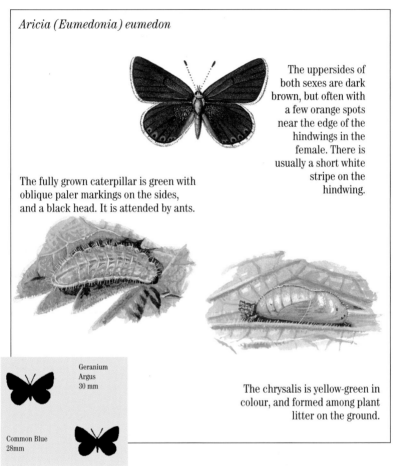

Aricia (Eumedonia) eumedon

The uppersides of both sexes are dark brown, but often with a few orange spots near the edge of the hindwings in the female. There is usually a short white stripe on the hindwing.

The fully grown caterpillar is green with oblique paler markings on the sides, and a black head. It is attended by ants.

Geranium Argus 30 mm

Common Blue 28mm

The chrysalis is yellow-green in colour, and formed among plant litter on the ground.

Favoured habitats are woodland clearings and flowery meadows in mountainous areas in southern and central Europe, but at lower altitudes in the north. In the flower-rich meadows of southern Scandinavia they can be very abundant. There is a very close association with cranesbills, as the eggs are laid on the flowers or upper leaves of various species of geranium, and the adult butterflies take nectar and also rest on them. Courtship and mating also frequently take place around the middle of the day on the geranium flowers. Where cranesbills are abundant, the butterflies are often present in large numbers. While sunbathing or feeding, the butterflies are easily approached, and rarely fly far when disturbed. The young caterpillars feed on the fruits of the food plant, and the winter is spent in this stage.

A Geranium Argus shows its underside. Note the pattern of spots: no spot between the body and the central spot on the forewing, and the central spot on the hindwing with a white streak. The greenish scales close to the body on the hindwing are also typical.

WHERE Sometimes common, but locally distributed in southern and south-eastern Europe and in Scandinavia. It is absent from Britain.

WHEN There is one generation a year, flying mainly in late June and July.

LOOKALIKES

The **Brown Argus** (page 88) and its relatives are similar, but nearly always have better-developed orange markings on both underside and upperside.

Brown Argus

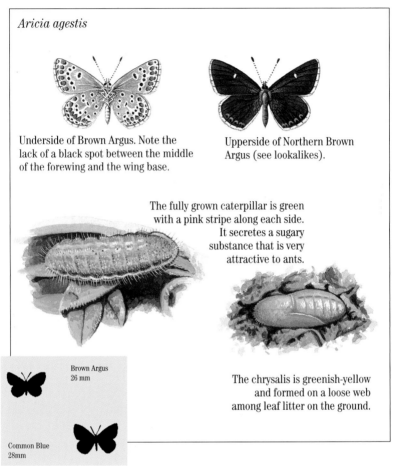

Aricia agestis

Underside of Brown Argus. Note the lack of a black spot between the middle of the forewing and the wing base.

Upperside of Northern Brown Argus (see lookalikes).

The fully grown caterpillar is green with a pink stripe along each side. It secretes a sugary substance that is very attractive to ants.

The chrysalis is greenish-yellow and formed on a loose web among leaf litter on the ground.

Brown Argus
26 mm

Common Blue
28mm

Both sexes are dark brown with orange marginal markings on the upperside. In the females these are usually more prominent than in the males. The underside is greyish or pale brown, with black spots and an orange border, but often looks silver-grey when the butterfly is in flight. The strongholds of this butterfly are chalk and limestone grasslands where the turf is kept short. Here the eggs are laid on leaves of rock-rose (*Helianthemum*). Other habitats are frequently colonized, too, including set-aside fields, roadside verges and disturbed ground where cranesbills and storksbills are used as food plants for the caterpillars. Although the butterflies tend to fly only short distances, they have good ability to disperse and colonize new sites. The winter is spent as a small caterpillar.

A female basks on a campion flower. The even row of orange spots around the wing margins and the absence of a blue flush near the base of the wings are distinctive. The white edged black spot on the forewing is more typical of some forms of the Northern Brown Argus.

WHERE Widespread and often common throughout Europe, but absent from northern Britain, and all but the southern tip of Scandinavia.

WHEN Three generations a year in southern Europe, where adults can be seen from April to October. Further north usually has two flight periods: May-June and late July to August.

LOOKALIKES

The **Northern Brown Argus** (*Aricia artaxerxes*) is typically larger, and the orange spots are usually reduced. It flies in mountains and in northern Europe. The **Brown Argus** is often confused with the female **Common Blue** (see page 108).

Alpine Blue/Glandon Blue

Alpine Blue
Plebejus (Albulina) orbitulus

Glandon Blue
Plebejus (Agriades) glandon

Underside of Alpine Blue. Note the lack of black spots on the hindwing.

Upperside of male Glandon Blue. The silver-grey colour and plain white wing fringes are distinctive.

Alpine Blue
26 mm
Glandon Blue
26 mm

The caterpillar of the Alpine Blue is green with vague paler markings.

The caterpillar of the Glandon Blue is green with a black line along its back and pink markings along its sides and back.

Common Blue
28mm

The male of the **Alpine Blue** is bright blue on the upperside, with a narrow black border and clear white fringes. The female is dark brown. The male **Glandon Blue** is silvery-grey on the upperside, also with a brown female. Both species have reduced black spotting on the underside hindwings, often showing as white patches. Both are mountain species, and can sometimes be seen together, drinking at moist patches along pathways. The caterpillars of the Alpine Blue feed on milk vetches and *Oxytropis*, those of the Glandon Blue on rock-jasmine (*Androsace species*) and saxifrages. In northern Scandinavia a unique form of the Glandon Blue (*aquilo*) lives on south-facing outcrops of shale and slate. Both species occur in exposed habitats, and spend much time at rest on sheltered paths, basking with open wings when the sun shines.

Alpine Blue
A male Alpine blue opens its wings to the sun while drinking moisture from the edge of a mountain path. Note the plain white fringes and narrow black border to the wings.

Glandon Blue
Two male Glandon Blues drink from a mountain path, with wings closed. Notice the absence of a central black spot in the hindwing, and reduction of some of the other spots, leaving small white patches.

WHERE AND WHEN
Flies in the Alps, and mountains of Scandinavia. On the wing in July and August.

Alpine Blue

Glandon Blue

WHERE AND WHEN
Flies in the Alps, also in the Pyrenees. Closely-related forms also occur in Scandinavia. On the wing in July and August, or earlier in Scandinavia.

Mazarine Blue

Polyommatus (Cyaniris) semiargus

The female is plain dark brown on the upperside, with white fringes, and sometimes a slight scattering of blue scales at the base of the wings.

The undersides of both sexes are pale greyish-brown with white-ringed black spots, and unmarked wing margins.

The caterpillar is green with a darker line along the back and obscure paler markings.

Mazarine Blue 32 mm

Common Blue 28mm

The chrysalis is brown, heavily mottled with darker brown markings.

The male upperside is violet-blue, with the veins narrowly outlined in black and a black border. The butterflies favour flowery meadows and occur from lowlands up to 2,200 m in mountains. The eggs are laid on the flower heads of red clover, kidney vetch or other small plants in the pea family, and the young caterpillars feed on the flowers and shoots. They spend the winter as caterpillars, and in spring resume feeding on the young leaves of the clover. They are able to secrete a sugar solution which is attractive to ants. Like many other blue species this association with ants is believed to offer protection from parasites and predators. The Mazarine Blue became extinct as a breeding species in Britain early in the 20th Century, and is threatened in lowland Europe by loss of flower-rich grassland and the decline in cultivation of clover.

A male Mazarine Blue basks with open wings. The blue ground colour is rather dark, and the width of the darker border is quite variable. The distinctive feature is the way the wing veins are narrowly outlined in black.

WHERE Widespread and often common in suitable habitats throughout Europe, including Scandinavia. Extinct in Britain.

WHEN There may be one or two generations in a year, and the butterfly may be seen from May to August or September, depending on locality.

LOOKALIKES

The unmarked borders of the undersides are distinctive in both sexes, and the black outlining of the veins on the male upperside are distinctive.

Damon Blue

Polyommatus (Agrodiaetus) damon

The dark brown upperside of the female, sometimes with a blue flush around the base of the wings.

Underside of female. Note the distinctive white stripe.

The caterpillar is green with a darker line along its back and pink lines along its sides.

The chrysalis is pale green or olive brown, and formed among leaf litter.

Damon Blue
30 mm

Common Blue
28mm

This butterfly is found in flowery meadows from medium altitudes up to 2,400 m in mountains. The pale blue upperside of the male shines silvery or turquoise as it moves in bright sunlight. The dark borders are wide and ill-defined, partially extending along the veins. The undersides of both sexes are brown, usually darker in the females, with black spots and a prominent white stripe. The butterflies are closely associated with sainfoins, often sipping nectar from their flowers and using them as the food plant of their caterpillars. The females spend most of their time nectaring, resting on flower heads or laying their pale-greenish eggs on flowers or friuts of the sainfoin. The males bask with open wings, and often drink from damp patches on the ground. The winter is spent as an egg or young caterpillar.

A male Damon Blue, wings partly open, shows the white underside stripe. The upperside is iridescent turquoise with a wide, ill-defined dark border. The only other widespread species with a blue male and an underside white stripe is the Furry Blue.

WHERE Localised, but in some places common, in southern, central and eastern Europe.

WHEN It flies in the latter half of July, through August and later.

LOOKALIKES

The females could be mistaken for those of **Ripart's Anomalous Blue** (page 98) or the **Furry Blue** (page 96) but the underside ground colour of the female Damon Blue is usually much darker than in the other two.

Furry Blue

Polyommatus (Agrodiaetus) dolus

Brown upperside of female.

Underside of female Furry Blue. The white stripe on the hindwing is variable, and sometimes absent.

The caterpillar is pale green with markings on the back and sides and an orange-brown line along each side. It feeds on sanfoin.

The chrysalis is pale yellowish-brown and formed on the ground among leaf litter.

Furry Blue
33 mm

Common Blue
28mm

The male's upperside is a pale shining silvery-blue, but with an extensive rough 'furry' area at the base of the forewing. During courtship this area releases pheromones that attract the female. The male's underside is pale grey-brown, the female usually darker brown, and both have white-ringed black spots and usually a white stripe on the hindwing. The butterflies are sedentary, spending most of their time taking nectar from flowers such as lavender and eryngo and for most of the day they do so with their wings closed. The striking upperside of the male is most likely to be seen when the first rays of the sun reach the habitat in early morning. In south-eastern France the butterfly occurs in open areas among shrubs or light woodland, and in the Cevennes it flies on large areas of dry grassland and hillsides.

A male Furry Blue opens its wings to the early morning sun. The shining silvery-blue resembles that of the Chalk-hill Blue, but it lacks the laddered wing fringes of that species. The rough patch of scent scales clearly visible on the forewings is also distinctive.

WHERE The Furry Blue has a discontinuous distribution in southern Europe, but can be locally common.

WHEN There is one generation in a year and the adults can be seen from mid-July to the end of August.

LOOKALIKES

The female of the **Damon Blue** (page 94) is darker brown on the underside, and the white stripe is more prominent. See also **Ripart's Anomalous Blue** (page 98).

Ripart's Anomalous Blue

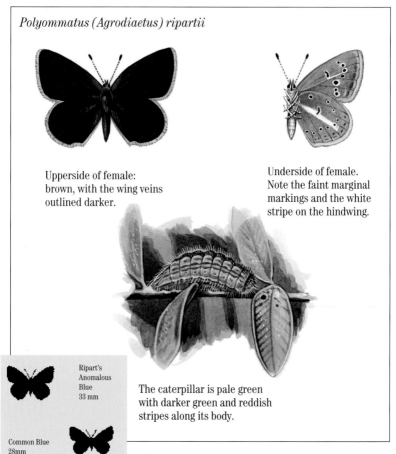

Polyommatus (Agrodiaetus) ripartii

Upperside of female:
brown, with the wing veins
outlined darker.

Underside of female.
Note the faint marginal
markings and the white
stripe on the hindwing.

Ripart's
Anomalous
Blue
33 mm

The caterpillar is pale green
with darker green and reddish
stripes along its body.

Common Blue
28mm

This is one of a group of similar anomalous blues that have brown
uppersides in the males, and, like the Furry Blue, areas of rough
scent scales on the forewings. The underside of the male is pale greyish-
brown and that of the female is usually somewhat darker. In both sexes
there is usually a white stripe along the underside hindwing. Most of the
day is spent at rest or feeding from flowers with the wings closed.
Lavender, eryngos and various species of mint are particularly favoured
as food plants. In the early morning, late afternoon or after a period of
dull weather the butterflies open their wings to bask. The eggs are laid
on the flowers of sainfoin, and the winter is spent as a small caterpillar.
In spring the caterpillar feeds on the sainfoin flowers and is usually
attended by ants.

A male basks with open wings, revealing the rough patch of scent scales on each forewing. Note the paler brown fringes to the wings and lack of upperside markings except for a darker outlining of the veins. The most widespread of the Anomalous Blue group.

WHERE Discontinuously distributed in southern and south-eastern Europe, but quite widespread in southern France.

WHEN The adults can be seen from the end of June until early August.

LOOKALIKES

Considerable experience is needed to separate the various species of Anomalous Blue. Ripart's Anomalous Blue females have pale brown fringes to their wings. These are white in female **Furry** (page 96) and **Damon** (page 94) blues.

Turquoise Blue

Polyommatus (Plebicula) dorylas

The female upperside is dark brown with orange spots around the wing edges, but often only a few on the hindwing only.

The underside is distinctive in both sexes as there is a white border between the orange spots and the wing edges.

The caterpillar is pale green with tiny white markings, and is often attended by ants.

The chrysalis is pale yellow and greenish, with a red-brown line along the back. It is formed on the ground.

Turquoise Blue
33 mm

Common Blue
28mm

The males of this species are very distinctive, with pale, shimmering blue-green uppersides. There is a narrow black border to the wings which extends a little way along the veins. The undersides of both sexes have distinctive white margins, especially on the forewings. The favoured habitats of this butterfly are warm, flowery meadows and open clearings in scrub, from medium altitude up to 2,200 m in mountains. The adult butterflies take nectar from thyme, eryngo, clover and various flowers in the pea family, and often settle with their wings open. The eggs are laid on the leaves of kidney vetch, and the winter is spent as a part-grown caterpillar. Ants of several species attend the caterpillar, and probably protect it from parasite attacks. The adult butterflies are quite easy to approach for photography.

A male perches on a seed head with wings partly open. The male catches the eye, with its unique pale, shimmering blue colour. There is a narrow black line around the wing margin, and the veins are partly outlined in black. The fringes are white.

WHERE Widely distributed in southern and central Europe, including the southern tip of Scandinavia, but absent from Britain and northern France.

WHEN Adults can be seen from May to September at low altitudes, where they have two generations in a year; in July and August at higher altitudes.

LOOKALIKES

The white border on the underside distinguishes it from similar species.

Meleager's Blue

Polyommatus (Meleageria) daphnis

The underside of the male is an even, pale fawn-grey with small black spots and faint markings around the margins.

The male is pale blue on the upperside with a black border on the forewing that shades into the blue, and extends part-way along the wing veins.

Female upperside form *steeveni* (See below).

The caterpillar is pale green, with two yellow bands bordered by darker green along the back.

Meleager's Blue 34 mm

Common Blue 28mm

There are two quite different colour forms of the female, one with silver-blue areas on the upperside (opposite), the other mainly brown (form *steeveni*, above). The latter is the dominant form in more southerly populations. The female underside is deeper brown and more strongly marked than that of the male. Both sexes have a distinctive wavy hind-edge to the hindwing, more obvious in the female. The butterflies inhabit warm, dry grasslands and feed from thistles, thyme and other flowers in the mint family. The females lay their pale greenish eggs singly on the leaves of crown vetch. The winter is spent in the egg stage or as a newly-hatched caterpillar on the foliage. In spring the caterpillar feeds on the leaves of the vetch, and is attended by ants. The chrysalis is formed on the ground among leaf-litter.

A female sips from a flower, with wings half open. The strongly scalloped margin to the hindwing is unique. The silvery blue 'rays' on both fore- and hindwings are also distinctive, but in parts of the southern range females have mainly brown uppersides.

WHERE Widely distributed in southern and central Europe

WHEN One generation in a year; the adult butterflies can be seen from the middle of June though July and August.

LOOKALIKES

The shape of the hindwings and lack of orange markings on the underside should separate this species from all others.

Chalk-hill Blue

Polyommatus (Lysandra) coridon

The underside of the male is pale grey with black spots and faint orange spots near the edge of the hindwings.

The upperside of the female is usually dark brown on the upperside with orange marginal spots, especially on the hindwings.

Upperside of a female of form *syngrapha* (see below).

The caterpillar is green with two lines of yellow spots along its back and a yellow line along each side.

Chalk-hill Blue 35 mm

Common Blue 28mm

The chrysalis is pale yellow-brown, with a darker line along its back.

The female underside is similar to that of the male, but the ground colour is pale brown. The colour of the males varies considerably in different parts of Europe, and there are variant forms of the female with blue uppersides (for example f. *syngrapha*). The favoured habitat is chalk and limestone downland where the caterpillar's food-plant, horse-shoe vetch, grows. The species is threatened by the ploughing up of its grassland habitats in some areas. Elsewhere, lack of grazing by sheep or rabbits leads to the shading out of the caterpillar's food-plant. The eggs are laid on or close to plants of horseshoe vetch, and the winter is usually spent in this stage. In spring the caterpillar feeds by night on horseshoe vetch. It is attended by ants and forms its chrysalis in the ants' nest.

A male basks on a flower with wings wide spread. This species often shares its grassland habitat with the Adonis Blue, and the two may fly together in August. The pale silvery-blue upperside combined with the laddered wing fringes are distinctive.

WHERE Widespread throughout Europe, but absent from northern Britain, Scandinavia and southern Spain.

WHEN In most areas there is one generation in a year. The adults can be seen in July and August.

LOOKALIKES

The Provençal **Chalk-hill Blue** (*Polyammatus hispana*) flies in the south. The male is paler on the upperside; the female is almost identical to that of the Chalk-hill Blue. South-east and south-west Europe have other similar species.

Adonis Blue

Polyommatus (Lysandra) bellargus

The upperside of the female is dark brown with a variable number of orange markings around the margins. Note the blue scales at the margins of the hindwings.

The underside of a female.

The caterpillar is dark green with two lines of yellow spots along the back and yellow lines along the sides.

Adonis Blue
32 mm

Common Blue
28 mm

The upperside of the male is brilliant blue, shining turquoise as the wings catch the sun in flight. There is a narrow black marginal line and the white fringes are laddered with black as in the Chalk-hill Blue. The underside of the male is pale brown but otherwise the undersides are similar to those of the Chalk-hill Blue. The butterfly inhabits flowery grasslands where the caterpillar's food plant is abundant, but in the northern part of its range requires the high temperatures provided by short turf on south-facing downland slopes. The caterpillars feed on all parts of the plants of horseshoe vetch, and are attended by ants that protect them from parasitic attack in return for the sugary solution which they secrete. The species is threatened by ploughing of downland and by lack of grazing elsewhere.

A male Adonis Blue basks with its wings spread wide. It is almost impossible to capture on film the iridescent turquoise-blue of this spectacular butterfly, but once seen it is unmistakable. The black-and-white laddered wing fringes are also distinctive.

WHERE Widespread where its habitat exists throughout Europe, except northern Britain and Scandinavia.

WHEN There are usually two generations in a year. The adults fly in May and June, and again from late July to September.

LOOKALIKES

The females are similar to those of the **Chalk-hill Blue** (page 104), but have blue scales at the outer margin of the hindwings (white in the Chalk-hill Blue). Male **Common Blues** (page 108) have plain white fringes (laddered in the Adonis).

Common Blue

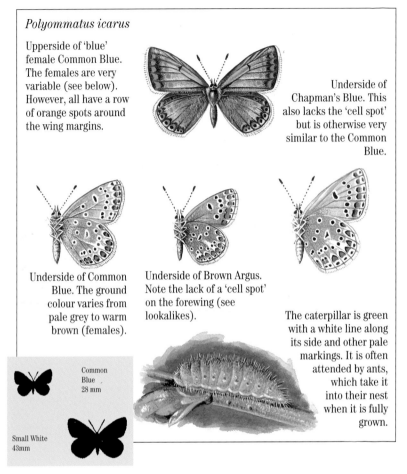

Polyommatus icarus

Upperside of 'blue' female Common Blue. The females are very variable (see below). However, all have a row of orange spots around the wing margins.

Underside of Chapman's Blue. This also lacks the 'cell spot' but is otherwise very similar to the Common Blue.

Underside of Common Blue. The ground colour varies from pale grey to warm brown (females).

Underside of Brown Argus. Note the lack of a 'cell spot' on the forewing (see lookalikes).

The caterpillar is green with a white line along its side and other pale markings. It is often attended by ants, which take it into their nest when it is fully grown.

Common Blue 28 mm

Small White 43mm

The Common Blue is a familiar inhabitant of rough grassland, roadside verges, meadows and brownfield sites, wherever the food plants of its caterpillars thrive. These are small plants in the pea family, most notably bird's-foot trefoils, clovers, medicks and restharrow. Males are bright blue on the upperside, usually with a violet tint, and paler blue outlining of the wing veins. They often congregate in large numbers, and are a beautiful sight as they bask with their wings open to the sun. After a period of basking late in the day, they settle with their wings closed and heads down on long grass stems. The females are usually brown on the upperside, with variable amounts of blue scaling. They are less conspicuous than the males, and spend much of their time either drinking nectar from flowers or laying their eggs on leaf tips.

A male basks on horseshoe vetch. During the hottest part of the day, males almost constantly perform a dancing flight in search of females. Early or late in the day, or as the sun comes out after poor weather, they face the sun with open wings.

WHERE Widespread and often common throughout Europe, from sea level to 2,500 m.

WHEN In southern Europe can complete two, three or even four generations a year, flying from March to November. In the far north and at high altitudes it manages only one, flying in June and July.

LOOKALIKES

The Common Blue has a black 'cell spot' near the base of the underside forewing. This is missing in other similar species, such as the **Brown Argus** (page 88), **Chapman's Blue** (*P. thersites*) and **Escher's Blue** (*P. escheri*).

109

Eros Blue

Polyommatus eros

Upperside of female: brown on the upperside, with weakly marked orange spots round the margins.

Underside. Note the 'cell spot' on the forewing, as in the Common Blue.

The caterpillar is green with yellowish lines along the back and sides. As with many blues, they are attended by ants.

Eros Blue
28 mm

Common Blue
28 mm

The Eros Blue flies in mountains, usually above 1,500 m, where the males often congregate in large numbers to drink from damp patches on the ground. Courtship and mating also often occur in these places. The males have shining pale sky-blue uppersides that glisten silver and turquoise in different lights. They have a black border round the wing margins that breaks up into black spots on the hindwings. The pattern of spots on the underside is similar to that of the Common Blue, but usually less prominent. The eggs are laid on the leaves of milk-vetches (*Oxytropis* species), on which the caterpillars feed. The winter is spent as a small caterpillar. Males frequently bask with wings open, on low-growing vegetation. A very striking form (*menelaos*) occurs in the Taygetos mountains of southern Greece.

A male drinks from a muddy path. Males of many blue species sip from damp ground, gaining trace nutrients and water. The distinctive pale turquoise-blue upperside shows well here: it looks different in other lights. Note black wing border and white fringes.

WHERE Flies in the Alps, Pyrenees and some other European mountain ranges.

WHEN There is just one generation in the year, and the adults are most likely to be seen in July and August.

LOOKALIKES

The presence of the 'cell spot' on the underside forewing separates it from other similar species. Colour and the black margins separate the males from those of the **Common Blue** (page 108).

Duke of Burgundy

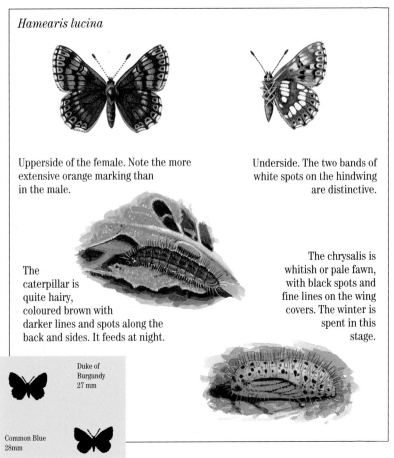

Hamearis lucina

Upperside of the female. Note the more extensive orange marking than in the male.

Underside. The two bands of white spots on the hindwing are distinctive.

The caterpillar is quite hairy, coloured brown with darker lines and spots along the back and sides. It feeds at night.

The chrysalis is whitish or pale fawn, with black spots and fine lines on the wing covers. The winter is spent in this stage.

Duke of Burgundy 27 mm

Common Blue 28mm

This butterfly is the sole member of its group - the 'metalmarks' - in Europe. Because of the orange and black lattice pattern on the upperside, it has been associated with the fritillaries, but it is more closely related to the blues. The main food plants of the caterpillars are cowslip and primrose (other *Primula* species are also used in some areas), and the species forms small colonies where these plants grow in tussocky grassland on chalk or limestone, or in open areas in woodland. The males are territorial, spending much time on a favoured perch, flying off to chase off another butterfly or court a passing female. The females cover considerable distances as they search for suitable plants on which to lay their eggs. The survival of the butterfly is threatened by a combination of changes in forestry management and loss of its downland habitats.

A male Duke of Burgundy basks in the morning sun in a woodland ride. The hindwings have only small orange spots (in contrast with the Chequered Skipper). Shading of the habitat by tall conifers finally extinguished this colony.

WHERE Still widespread in suitable habitats through Europe except for the far south and north Scandinavia. It is very localized in north Britain.

WHEN Two generations a year in most of Europe, on the wing from April to September. In more northerly localities there is just one flight period from late April to mid-June.

LOOKALIKES

It is much smaller than the fritillaries, and has a distinctive underside pattern. It is similar in general appearance to the **Chequered Skipper** (page 240), but the pattern on the upperside hindwing is clearly different.

Two-tailed Pasha

Charaxes jasius

The underside with its mottled brown-orange and blue pattern and white stripe, is unmistakable.

The fully grown caterpillar is green with 'eye' markings on its back, a yellow stripe along each side, and four reddish 'horns' on its head.

Two-tailed Pasha
65 mm

Small White
43mm

The chrysalis is stout, pale green and usually suspended from a leaf or stem of the strawberry tree.

This magnificent butterfly favours hot, dry scrubland with an abundance of the caterpillar's food plant: the strawberry tree. They fly powerfully, and the whirring of their wings is audible. There are two 'tails' on each hindwing, and the upperside is deep chocolate brown with orange margins, and a row of blue spots on the hindwing. The adults spend much of their time around the branches of the strawberry tree but also seek out the decaying pods of the carob tree or other fermenting fruits. It is said that they can be lured to alcoholic drinks. Except when feeding, they are alert and difficult to approach. The eggs are laid singly on the leaves of the strawberry tree, and the resulting caterpillars are superbly camouflaged. Eggs laid in spring produce a new generation in late summer. The winter is spent as a caterpillar.

A Two-tailed Pasha feeds with open wings from rotting fruit on the ground. The upperside is less often seen in living specimens. The pattern of dark chocolate-brown with orange-yellow borders and double 'tails' at the rear of each hindwing is unique.

WHERE This is a southern species, but quite widespread, especially around Mediterranean coasts and islands.

WHEN Two generations each year, in May and June, and again from mid-August into the autumn.

LOOKALIKES

No other European butterfly has this combination of size, underside pattern and double 'tails'.

Purple Emperor

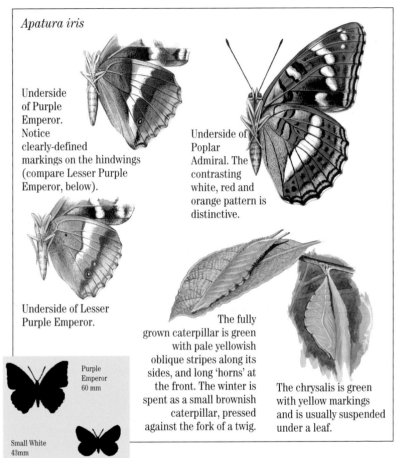

Apatura iris

Underside of Purple Emperor. Notice clearly-defined markings on the hindwings (compare Lesser Purple Emperor, below).

Underside of Poplar Admiral. The contrasting white, red and orange pattern is distinctive.

Underside of Lesser Purple Emperor.

Purple Emperor 60 mm

Small White 43mm

The fully grown caterpillar is green with pale yellowish oblique stripes along its sides, and long 'horns' at the front. The winter is spent as a small brownish caterpillar, pressed against the fork of a twig.

The chrysalis is green with yellow markings and is usually suspended under a leaf.

The Purple Emperor is one of the most strikingly beautiful of all the European butterflies. The uppersides of both males and females are dark brown with irregular white bands. The male alone has the brilliant purple sheen, visible when the light strikes the wings from certain angles. The habitat is mature woodland, and the males congregate high up around the canopy of a tall 'master' tree. Females also visit these trees, and after mating they descend to lower levels to lay their eggs on the leaves of sallow or willow bushes – especially broad-leaved sallows growing in shade. The males come down to feed from puddles, faeces or decaying matter, occasionally opening their wings as they do so. Otherwise, despite their striking appearance, their presence in a wood can easily be overlooked.

A male drinks from damp soil. This may help them acquire salts useful in the synthesis of pheromones; they also feed from decaying organic matter. The purple sheen covers most of the upperside, but is only visible when light is reflected from certain angles.

WHERE Across Europe, but absent from most of Spain and Italy, and from all but the southern tip of Scandinavia. In Britain, confined to wooded areas in the south.

WHEN One generation a year. On the wing late June through July and into August. Early July is the best time to look for the males on the ground.

LOOKALIKES

Lesser Purple Emperor (*Apatura ilia*) is very similar, but has well-defined orange-ringed black spots on the forewing. The **Poplar Admiral** (*Limenitis populi*) lacks the purple sheen. See also **White Admiral** (page 118).

White Admiral/Southern White Admiral

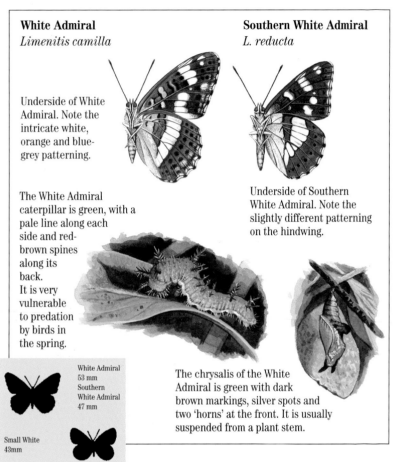

White Admiral
Limenitis camilla

Southern White Admiral
L. reducta

Underside of White Admiral. Note the intricate white, orange and blue-grey patterning.

Underside of Southern White Admiral. Note the slightly different patterning on the hindwing.

The White Admiral caterpillar is green, with a pale line along each side and red-brown spines along its back.
It is very vulnerable to predation by birds in the spring.

White Admiral
53 mm
Southern
White Admiral
47 mm

Small White
43mm

The chrysalis of the White Admiral is green with dark brown markings, silver spots and two 'horns' at the front. It is usually suspended from a plant stem.

The **White Admiral** is one of the most graceful of the woodland butterflies, as it glides along open rides, stopping occasionally to bask in a sun spot, or take nectar from bramble blossom. It often feeds with open wings, showing off the contrasting black and white pattern of the upperside, but when it closes them the intricate patterning of the underside is revealed. The females lay their eggs singly on the leaves of honeysuckle growing in shade.

The **Southern White Admiral** is more often found in open shrubby woodland and sunny hillsides. It is very similar to the White Admiral but has a blue sheen on the upperside, and a white spot in the middle of each forewing. This species also lays its eggs on the leaves of plants in the honeysuckle group. Both species spend the winter as small caterpillars.

White Admiral

Two White Admirals feed from bramble blossom, displaying their striking black and white uppersides. Owing to their fondness for bramble flowers, their wings soon become tattered.

*A **Southern White Admiral** basks with wings wide open. Note the white spot near the middle of the leading edge of the forewing: this is absent in the White Admiral. The blue sheen reflects light at certain angles and shimmers in the sun.*

WHERE AND WHEN
The White Admiral is widespread in Europe, but absent from the far south and also from northern Britain and most of Scandinavia. Flies from late June through July into early August.

White Admiral

Southern White Admiral

WHERE AND WHEN
A more southerly distribution, and is absent from both Britain and Scandinavia. The flight period is July in the northern part of its range, but it has two broods in the south.

Camberwell Beauty

Nymphalis antiopa

The chrysalis is pale grey-brown with small flecks of black, and is usually suspended from a leaf or plant stem.

The underside is dark grey with fine black striations, and whitish margins.

Camberwell Beauty
62 mm

Small White
43mm

The fully grown caterpillar is black with long black spines, tiny white points and red patches along its back. It is vulnerable to parasite attack.

This is primarily a woodland butterfly, but it flies powerfully and disperses widely. It can be seen in parks, gardens and hedgerows in cultivated land. The upperside is a rich chocolate brown in colour with pale yellow margins, and a row of bright blue spots. The margins soon become tattered and after hibernation have usually faded to white. In spring they are often attracted to sallow catkins, and later in the year feed from bramble, hemp agrimony and other flowers. However, they are particularly attracted to tree sap, decaying fruit, and to damp patches of soil. The eggs are laid in rings around a branch of sallow, poplar or aspen. The resulting caterpillars stay together protected by a web of silk. They practise a collective warning movement that deters predators. Later they feed separately. The winter is spent as an adult.

A Camberwell Beauty drinks from a damp woodland path. This probably gives them trace nutrients as well as water, but they also drink sap from tree trunks and visit flowers such as thistles, hemp agrimony and buddleia to build up their reserves for hibernation.

WHERE Widespread throughout Europe, but less common in the northern part of its range, and represented only by occasional migrants in Britain.

WHEN Adults can be seen in spring and early summer; the new brood appears from June or July onwards, depending on locality.

LOOKALIKES

No other European butterfly has a similar pattern and colour on the upperside.

Small Tortoiseshell/Large Tortoiseshell

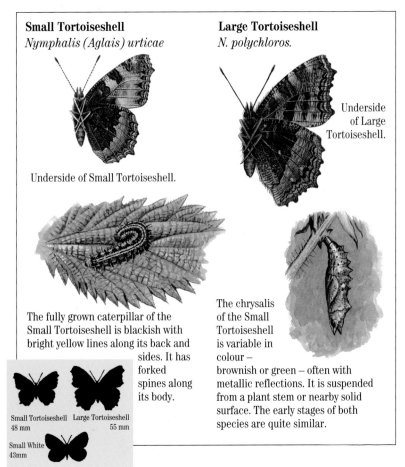

Small Tortoiseshell
Nymphalis (Aglais) urticae

Large Tortoiseshell
N. polychloros.

Underside
of Large
Tortoiseshell.

Underside of Small Tortoiseshell.

The fully grown caterpillar of the Small Tortoiseshell is blackish with bright yellow lines along its back and sides. It has forked spines along its body.

The chrysalis of the Small Tortoiseshell is variable in colour – brownish or green – often with metallic reflections. It is suspended from a plant stem or nearby solid surface. The early stages of both species are quite similar.

Small Tortoiseshell
48 mm

Large Tortoiseshell
55 mm

Small White
43mm

The **Small Tortoiseshell** is one of the most familiar European butterflies, and one of the first to be seen basking in spring sunshine after hibernation. It occurs wherever its caterpillar's food plant – stinging nettle – grows, often in neglected gardens and wasteland in urban areas. The butterflies disperse widely and can even be seen flying on mountain tops. They hibernate in crevices in trees or in buildings.

The **Large Tortoiseshell** is usually larger and very similar, but its ground colour is yellowish rather than reddish-orange, and the black basal area of the hindwing is much less extensive than in the Small Tortoiseshell. The female carefully places her eggs in a neat cluster on a twig of the caterpillar's food plant. The resulting caterpillars live gregariously in a loose web. They are vulnerable to parasite attacks.

Upperside of Small Tortoiseshell.
A Small Tortoiseshell basks in summer sunshine. The following spring, after hibernation, they are often worn and faded. Notice the white patch close to the tip of the forewing.

Large Tortoiseshell.
A freshly emerged Large Tortoiseshell basks on a rock. Note the extra black spot on the forewing and absence of white patch near the tip.

WHERE AND WHEN
The Small Tortoiseshell is common and widespread throughout Europe. It can be seen in spring, with a fresh generation from July onwards.

Small Tortoiseshell

Large Tortoiseshell

WHERE AND WHEN
The Large Tortoiseshell is also very widespread but less common. In Scandinavia it is present only in the south, and is probably extinct as a breeding species in Britain.

Peacock

Nymphalis (Inachis) io

Underside: the dark colour and ragged outline of the wings provide excellent camouflage in their winter hiding places.

The chrysalis is pale yellow-green, with brown shading, and raised points along its back. It is suspended from a nettle stem or from some nearby solid surface.

The caterpillars feed together in groups on webs. When fully grown they are spiny, and velvet-black with white spots.

Peacock 60 mm

Small White 43mm

The Peacock is one of the most attractive and familiar of all European butterflies. The rich red-brown ground colour of the uppersides, combined with the brilliant blue and yellow 'eye' markings are striking and distinctive. After hibernation the males take up territories in sunny spots, often along a hedgerow or woodland ride. Here they bask with open wings, flying up to intercept passing females, or chase off other males. They also take time to sip nectar from spring flowers - sallow catkins are a particular favourite. The eggs are laid in batches on the undersides of the leaves of stinging nettles, and a new generation of adults emerges in the summer. These butterflies seek out nectar-rich flowers - often in parks and gardens - to build up their food stores for the long winter hibernation, often spent in hollow trees, woodpiles or buildings.

A freshly emerged Peacock settles on ragwort. The vivid 'eye' markings, set close to the wing tips, are thought to distract predators away from the vulnerable body of the insect. They may also act as a warning signal when the butterfly opens and closes its wings rapidly.

WHERE Widespread and usually common throughout Europe, absent only from the extreme south, and northern Scandinavia.

WHEN Hibernated individuals fly from March, overlapping with their offspring which emerge from June or July. These may fly until as late as October before entering hibernation.

LOOKALIKES

The prominent 'eye' markings on all four wings distinguish it from all other European butterflies.

Red Admiral

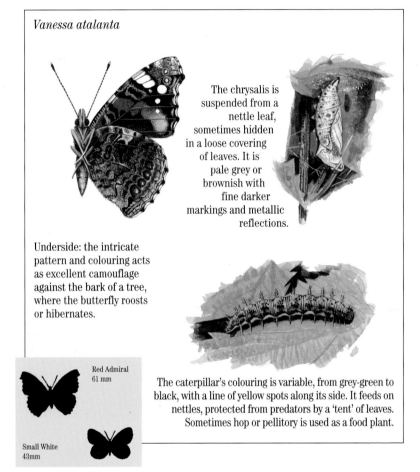

Vanessa atalanta

The chrysalis is suspended from a nettle leaf, sometimes hidden in a loose covering of leaves. It is pale grey or brownish with fine darker markings and metallic reflections.

Underside: the intricate pattern and colouring acts as excellent camouflage against the bark of a tree, where the butterfly roosts or hibernates.

Red Admiral
61 mm

Small White
43mm

The caterpillar's colouring is variable, from grey-green to black, with a line of yellow spots along its side. It feeds on nettles, protected from predators by a 'tent' of leaves. Sometimes hop or pellitory is used as a food plant.

The contrasting pattern of black with a red band on both wings and white spots towards the tip makes this one of the most distinctive butterflies. The underside, too, is beautifully but more subtly marked. The underside hindwing, especially, has a delicate tracery of browns, yellows, violet and blue. The sexes are very similar. In southern Europe there is usually a short period of hibernation before the butterflies mate and begin to migrate northwards, laying eggs and so starting new generations as they go. Their numbers build up until late summer, at which time they can be seen on a return, southerly migration. In northern Europe their populations are maintained by successive waves of migration, but there is increasing evidence that small numbers now survive the winter in southern Britain. The males establish and defend territories in spring.

A Red Admiral sips nectar from valerian flowers. The butterflies are unmistakable as they gather in summer on flowers of buddleia, Michaelmas daisy, dahlia or sedum, or drink from fermenting fruit. The flight is rapid and often quite erratic.

WHERE Owing to its migratory habit, the butterfly may be encountered throughout Europe, from sea level to mountain tops, though it is not fully resident in northern Europe.

WHEN Individuals can be seen at almost any time of year, but they are most abundant in mid- to late summer.

LOOKALIKES

The striking black, red and white upperside distinguishes it from all except the rare southern migrant **Indian Red Admiral** (*V. indica*).

Painted Lady

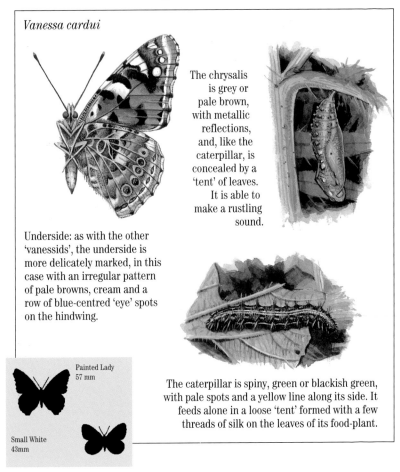

Vanessa cardui

The chrysalis is grey or pale brown, with metallic reflections, and, like the caterpillar, is concealed by a 'tent' of leaves. It is able to make a rustling sound.

Underside: as with the other 'vanessids', the underside is more delicately marked, in this case with an irregular pattern of pale browns, cream and a row of blue-centred 'eye' spots on the hindwing.

Painted Lady
57 mm

Small White
43mm

The caterpillar is spiny, green or blackish green, with pale spots and a yellow line along its side. It feeds alone in a loose 'tent' formed with a few threads of silk on the leaves of its food-plant.

The Painted Lady cannot survive the winter in most of mainland Europe, so the butterflies we see have either migrated from north Africa where they are permanent residents, or are descendants of such migrants. As they migrate northwards, some stop to breed on the way, and numbers build up during the spring and summer months. However, while migrating they are astonishingly direct and determined, sometimes flying in great numbers over mountains and other barriers. Eggs may be laid on many plant species, but most commonly on thistles. In some 'invasion' years, Painted Ladies can arrive in very large numbers in northern Europe, when they can be seen along with Red Admirals and Peacocks on buddleia and other ornamental shrubs in urban parks and gardens.

A Painted Lady drinks nectar from garden flowers. The butterflies are easily approached as they feed from garden flowers such as buddleia and valerian, but when disturbed have a powerful, gliding flight.

WHERE The Painted Lady migrates from its Mediterranean or Middle Eastern strongholds to reach virtually all Europe. There are occasional years of great abundance.

WHEN Reaches southern Europe in early spring; the north by May. Most abundant in July and August, but can be seen until October in most years.

LOOKALIKES

The pink to tawny-brown ground colour with black and white markings is distinctive.

Comma

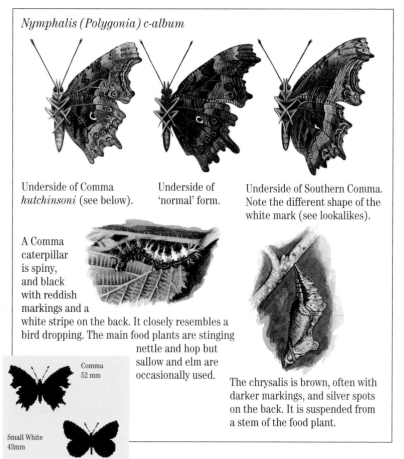

Nymphalis (Polygonia) c-album

Underside of Comma *hutchinsoni* (see below).

Underside of 'normal' form.

Underside of Southern Comma. Note the different shape of the white mark (see lookalikes).

A Comma caterpillar is spiny, and black with reddish markings and a white stripe on the back. It closely resembles a bird dropping. The main food plants are stinging nettle and hop but sallow and elm are occasionally used.

Comma
52 mm

Small White
43mm

The chrysalis is brown, often with darker markings, and silver spots on the back. It is suspended from a stem of the food plant.

The Comma has two main colour forms. The 'normal' form has a rich orange-brown ground colour on the upperside, with black markings, and an underside which is very dark brown to black, with bronze-green markings. The other form (*hutchinsoni*) is much paler, with yellow-orange uppersides, and paler fawn-brown undersides. The underside of the pale form can be beautifully variegated, with metallic green and lilac scales. Both forms have a white 'c' shaped mark on the underside. The darker form spends the winter hiding in crevices or among dead leaves, and in early spring can be seen sunbathing on bare patches of ground. Some of its offspring are of the pale form, and they go on to produce a second generation that emerges in late summer. These are of the dark form, and they soon enter hibernation. The males are territorial.

A Comma feeds on water mint in late summer, building up its food reserves for winter hibernation. Commas, with their characteristic jagged wing shape, are often seen at this time of year feeding from garden flowers, or from overripe fruit (especially blackberries).

WHERE Widespread and often common throughout Europe, except for Scotland, Ireland and northern Scandinavia.

WHEN Seen from March onwards, following hibernation, with later broods appearing from late May until Autumn.

LOOKALIKES

The **Southern Comma** (*N. egea*) is similar, but has a 'v' shaped mark in place of the 'c', and reduced dark markings on the upperside. In Europe it is confined to the south.

Map

Araschnia levana

The underside is very distinctive with an intricate pattern of white lines, broader pale bands, and often lilac patches on a darker background.

The greenish eggs are laid in strings, one on top of the other, on the underside of a nettle leaf.

The caterpillars are spiny and black or brown with broken yellow lines along the sides and back. They feed together on the leaves of nettle.

The chrysalis is brown or greenish-brown, often with metallic reflections. It is suspended from a leaf or plant stem. The winter is spent in this stage.

Map
42 mm

Small White
43mm

The Map is a common butterfly of woodland edges and clearings and shrubby areas, often in the damper parts of the habitat. It is unusual in having dramatically different spring and summer broods. The upperside of summer specimens is mainly black, with white markings. The differences are the result of the influence of weather conditions on the developing caterpillars. The butterflies of the spring brood are less common, and fly low, stopping frequently to bask in sunshine. Those of the later generation are particularly attracted to the flowers of hemp agrimony and bramble, and are more approachable than the spring brood. The males are territorial and will engage other passing males in a high, twirling flight, before returning to a favoured perch. The method of egg laying (see above) is unique.

The spring form is orange with irregular black markings, while the summer form is mainly black with white markings. On the upperside it resembles a White Admiral, but is much smaller.

WHERE Occurs in a wide swathe across Europe, but is absent from most of Italy and Spain in the south, and from Britain and most of Scandinavia in the north.

WHEN There are usually two generations in a year, with adults flying in May and June, and again in July and August.

LOOKALIKES

The summer form resembles a small **White Admiral**, but the underside is quite unlike that of any other European butterfly.

Silver-washed Fritillary

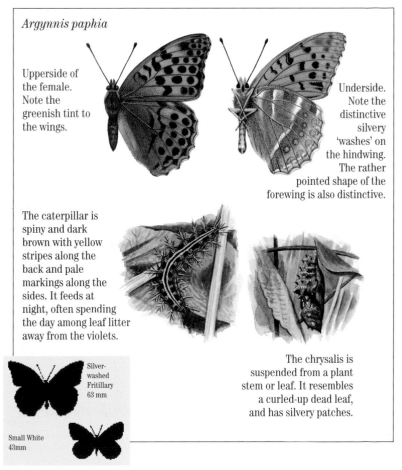

Argynnis paphia

Upperside of the female. Note the greenish tint to the wings.

Underside. Note the distinctive silvery 'washes' on the hindwing. The rather pointed shape of the forewing is also distinctive.

The caterpillar is spiny and dark brown with yellow stripes along the back and pale markings along the sides. It feeds at night, often spending the day among leaf litter away from the violets.

Silver-washed Fritillary 63 mm

The chrysalis is suspended from a plant stem or leaf. It resembles a curled-up dead leaf, and has silvery patches.

Small White 43mm

Except for the Cardinal this is the largest of the fritillaries. In suitable woodland habitats they can be abundant, and several may be seen on a single sprig of bramble flowers. The courtship flight is a spectacular aerobatic display, during which chemical scents (pheromones) are released from the streaks of black scaling along the forewing veins of the male. The female lacks these scent marks. After mating she searches for suitable places to lay her eggs. She first tests the ground under a tree to ensure there are enough violet flowers for the future caterpillars and then lays her eggs in crannies in the trunk of the tree. When the caterpillars hatch, they eat their eggshells, then remain on the tree through the winter. In spring, they crawl to the ground and begin to feed on the leaves of the violets. A minority of females have deep green uppersides (form *valezina*).

A male drinks nectar from flowers in a glade. This large, tawny butterfly is unmistakable as it swoops and glides along a woodland ride, or shows its green and silver underside as it drinks from bramble or thistle flowers. Note the black scent marks on the forewing.

WHERE This is one of the most widespread fritillaries, occurring throughout Europe except northern Britain and northern Scandinavia.

WHEN The butterfly has a long flight period, from July (June in the south) through to September.

LOOKALIKES

The Cardinal (*Argynnis pandora*) is larger, and has a rose-red flush on the underside of the forewing. The underside pattern distinguishes it from the other fritillaries.

Dark Green Fritillary

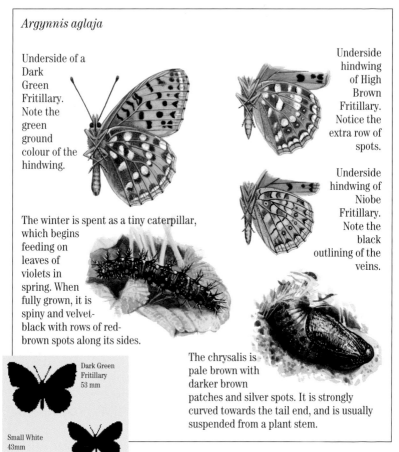

Argynnis aglaja

Underside of a Dark Green Fritillary. Note the green ground colour of the hindwing.

Underside hindwing of High Brown Fritillary. Notice the extra row of spots.

Underside hindwing of Niobe Fritillary. Note the black outlining of the veins.

The winter is spent as a tiny caterpillar, which begins feeding on leaves of violets in spring. When fully grown, it is spiny and velvet-black with rows of red-brown spots along its sides.

Dark Green Fritillary 53 mm

Small White 43mm

The chrysalis is pale brown with darker brown patches and silver spots. It is strongly curved towards the tail end, and is usually suspended from a plant stem.

The Dark Green Fritillary remains fairly common, although in many places the flower-rich open grasslands, moors, hillsides and coastal dune systems where it thrives are threatened by agricultural intensification and development pressures. The male has a rich tawny-brown ground colour to the upperside, while the female is slightly paler, often with yellowish spots along the wing margins. Sometimes, especially in the north, the females have a dark grey-green suffusion and more extensive black markings. The adults feed actively from thistles, scabious and other nectar-rich flowers, often opening and closing their wings as they do so. They are skittish and difficult to approach. The flight is swift and powerful, and they are known to be capable of flying several kilometres. The eggs are usually laid on dead vegetation close to patches of violets.

A male drinks nectar from a scabious flower. This large fritillary is often found on open heaths or downland, and has distinctive silver spots on a green background on its underside. The males have narrow lines of scent scales along the veins of the forewing.

WHERE In suitable habitats this fritillary can be found throughout Europe, including the far north of Scandinavia.

WHEN There is just one generation in a year, with adults flying from June (July in the north) to August.

LOOKALIKES

High Brown Fritillary (*Argynnis adippe*) and **Niobe Fritillary** (*A. niobe*) have a row of small reddish 'eye' spots on the underside hind-wing towards the outer margin. In Niobe the underside wing veins are finely outlined in black.

Queen of Spain Fritillary

Issoria lathonia

Upperside of female.

Underside. Note the striking pattern of very large silver spots on the hindwing. The outer edge of the forewings is concave, giving the wings an angular appearance.

The caterpillar is spiny and black with a double band of white spots along its back.

The chrysalis is suspended from a plant stem or leaf, and is dark brown or green, with white spots and a white band across the 'waist'. It resembles a bird dropping.

Queen of Spain Fritillary 45 mm

Small White 43mm

The Queen of Spain Fritillary inhabits a wide variety of flowery, open habitats, often, in the north, dunes and other coastal habitats. They have a migratory habit, but do not appear to fly as far as the Red Admiral and Painted Lady. The ground colour of the male upperside is orange-brown, as with other fritillaries, but the black markings tend to form distinct spots rather than a connected lattice. The females have a slightly paler ground colour, and often have a dark greenish suffusion around the wing bases (see above). The eggs are laid on the leaves of several species of pansies and violets, although it seems that northern populations use pansies more or less exclusively. The winter may be spent in any of the stages of its life history. When drinking nectar from a flower they are easily approached.

A male Queen of Spain Fritillary prepares to fly from its perch. The butterflies are fond of basking on bare ground or sipping nectar from thistles, knapweeds or eryngo. The very large silver spots on the underside, and the wing shape, are distinctive.

WHERE Widely distributed as a resident species throughout most of Europe, but in parts of its northern range it is represented by migrants only. Occasional migrants reach Britain.

WHEN Two, sometimes three, generations in a year. Adults can be seen from March to October.

LOOKALIKES

The very large silver spots on the underside and its angular wing shape distinguish it from all other European butterflies.

Marbled Fritillary

Brenthis daphne

Upperside of Marbled Fritillary. Usually a rich orange-brown in both sexes, with irregular black markings. A row of unevenly sized black spots runs through the outer part of both fore- and hindwings. Note the rounded shape of the wings.

Underside of Lesser Marbled Fritillary. Note the clear yellow patch arrowed. This is partly obscured by darker colours in the Marbled Fritillary (see the photograph).

The caterpillar is spiny and black with white markings, notably a double white line along the back.

The chrysalis is pale yellowish-white or grey with fine darker lines and metallic points.

Marbled Fritillary 45 mm

Small White 43mm

This is a medium-sized fritillary that may be seen in open woodland or shrubby grassland with abundant wildflowers. The underside is especially striking (see opposite), with yellow patches bordered with a thin brown lattice on the basal part of the hindwing and a cream, brown and lilac 'marbling' on the outer part of the wing. The wings are distinctly more rounded than those of other fritillaries. The butterflies are rather lazy fliers, and spend much of their time basking on the foliage of bushes with wings outspread, or sipping nectar from thistles or bramble blossom. The eggs are laid on the leaves of bramble or raspberry and the butterfly spends the winter as an egg or small caterpillar. The caterpillar feeds on leaves of bramble and related plants during the spring and early summer.

A Marbled Fritillary displays its intricately patterned underside as it sips nectar from a bramble flower. Compare the pattern of yellow patches with those on the Lesser Marbled Fritillary.

WHERE This butterfly is fairly widespread in south, central and eastern Europe, but absent from Britain and most of northern Europe.

WHEN There is one generation in a year and the adults are most likely to be seen in June and July.

LOOKALIKES

The **Lesser Marbled Fritillary** (*Brenthis ino*) is smaller, with a slight difference in the pattern of yellow underneath (see painting). The **Twin-spot Fritillary** (*B. hecate*) is also smaller, with rows of black spots on the upperside.

Mountain Fritillary

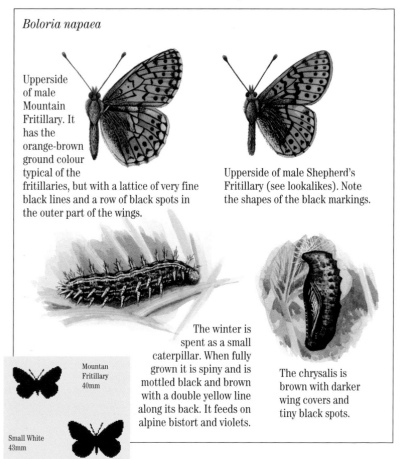

Boloria napaea

Upperside of male Mountain Fritillary. It has the orange-brown ground colour typical of the fritillaries, but with a lattice of very fine black lines and a row of black spots in the outer part of the wings.

Upperside of male Shepherd's Fritillary (see lookalikes). Note the shapes of the black markings.

The winter is spent as a small caterpillar. When fully grown it is spiny and is mottled black and brown with a double yellow line along its back. It feeds on alpine bistort and violets.

The chrysalis is brown with darker wing covers and tiny black spots.

Mountan Fritillary 40mm

Small White 43mm

This butterfly inhabits open, flowery slopes from the treeline upwards to 3000 metres in the Alps, and similar haunts at lower altitudes in Sweden and Norway. The upperside of the female is variable, but often has a greyish suffusion which reflects green and violet tints in certain lights. The hindwings are fawn with red-brown and white markings in the male, but with more subdued colouring in the female. The leading edge of the hindwings is almost straight, and makes a sharp angle with the outer edge. In sunny weather the males fly rapidly and tirelessly over the mountain slopes in search of females, and are very difficult to approach except in dull weather. The females are less active, resting with open wings among vegetation or taking nectar from flowers. The pale yellow eggs are laid singly on the foodplant.

A male rests with closed wings in cloudy weather. Note the shape of the hindwing and the colour match between its underside and the dead flower head. The hyperactive males become torpid as soon as the sun disappears behind a cloud and temperatures plummet

WHERE Discontinuous distribution. It flies at high altitudes in the Alps and Pyrenees, and at lower levels in Scandinavia.

WHEN Single, extended flight period from June to August. In the far north and at high altitudes development takes two years.

LOOKALIKES

The **Shepherd's Fritillary** (*Boloria pales*) often flies with the Mountain Fritillary. It has wider black markings: see painting. The **Cranberry Fritillary** (*B. aquilonaris*) is also similar, but has a redder underside.

Pearl-bordered Fritillary

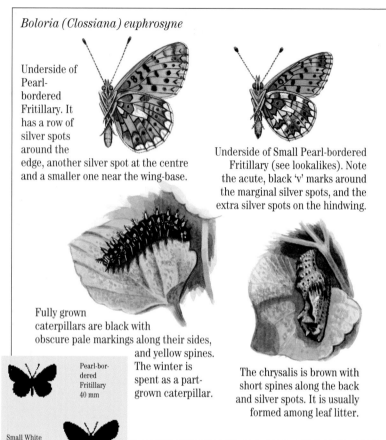

Boloria (Clossiana) euphrosyne

Underside of Pearl-bordered Fritillary. It has a row of silver spots around the edge, another silver spot at the centre and a smaller one near the wing-base.

Underside of Small Pearl-bordered Fritillary (see lookalikes). Note the acute, black 'v' marks around the marginal silver spots, and the extra silver spots on the hindwing.

Fully grown caterpillars are black with obscure pale markings along their sides, and yellow spines. The winter is spent as a part-grown caterpillar.

Pearl-bordered Fritillary 40 mm

Small White 43mm

The chrysalis is brown with short spines along the back and silver spots. It is usually formed among leaf litter.

This butterfly thrives in dry, south-facing hillsides with a mixture of grasses and bracken maintained by grazing animals, and in open rides and glades in woodland. Sheltered, sunny areas are chosen, and there must be a plentiful supply of the violets which are the food plants of the caterpillars. In many parts of Europe these habitats have been threatened by more intensive grassland management, conversion of old deciduous woodland to dense conifer plantations, and the decline of traditional woodland management. As the preferred habitats of the butterfly tend to become overgrown in a few years, they need to be able to colonise newly created patches of suitable habitat nearby. In Britain and some other European countries, habitat loss has seen numbers decline alarmingly. Eggs are laid on mossy stones or in leaf litter close to violets.

A male basks on thyme. The species flies low and swift along woodland edges or clearings, stopping to sip from woodland flowers. The Small Pearl-bordered Fritillary is the only similar species in these habitats, and darker forms (N. Europe) may cause confusion.

WHERE Throughout Europe, except for the extreme south-west, and often common where there is suitable habitat.

WHEN In much of Europe there are two generations a year: the first flies from April to June, the second emerges in August. In northern Europe, there is usually just one.

LOOKALIKES

The **Small Pearl-bordered Fritillary** (*B. selene*) usually has more silver spots on the underside hindwing, and the 'v' marks around the marginal silver spots are blacker and more sharply angled. See painting opposite.

Titania's Fritillary

Boloria (Clossiana) titania

Upperside of male Titania's Fritillary. Note the row of inward-pointing black triangles around the margins of the wings. These often fuse with an inner row of red-brown or black spots.

The caterpillar is black with yellow spines and two long, dark bristles pointing forward over its head.

The chrysalis is grey with black markings and is suspended from plant stems.

Titania's Fritillary 44 mm

Small White 43mm

This species inhabits subalpine meadows, flower-rich clearings and open woodland in mountains up to the treeline. They fly together with other species of fritillary, but are distinguished by the intricate pattern on the underside hindwing: patches and lines of fawn, red-brown, white and black are combined with a scattering of lilac scales. Their uppersides, too, are distinctive in having a row of black triangles pointing inwards around the wing margins. The females have rather paler undersides than the males, and western populations tend to have more subdued underside colouring. The eggs are laid on the caterpillar's food plant, which is usually bistort, but violets have also been reported. The winter is spent as an egg or small caterpillar. The butterflies are easily approached for photography.

A male rests with closed wings during inclement weather. The butterflies are attracted to yellow and purple flowers in the daisy family, such as leopard's bane, hawksbeards, knapweeds and thistles, which they use as platforms for basking as well as for feeding.

WHERE Discontinuous distribution: widespread in the Alps and Massif Central, and also occurring in the Balkans and around the Baltic, in north-east Europe.

WHEN One generation in a year, with the butterflies on the wing from June to August.

LOOKALIKES

The **Weaver's Fritillary** (*Clossiana dia*) is smaller and has a strongly angled hindwing.

Frejya's Fritillary

Boloria (Clossiana) freija

Upperside of male Frejya's Fritillary. Quite similar to the Pearl-bordered Fritillary, but the black spots tend to be more prominent and the basal area of the wings is suffused with dark scales.

Underside of Arctic Fritillary.

When fully grown the caterpillar is black with orange-yellow spines.

Underside of Frigga's Fritillary (see lookalikes).

Frejya's Fritillary 35 mm

Small White 43mm

Frejya's Fritillary inhabits boggy areas, forest clearings and tundra grasslands with low-growing vegetation. In its Arctic haunts it begins to fly a little earlier than most other species, and is often quite worn by the time they appear. The underside hindwing is distinctive with its complex pattern of white, fawn and red-brown with black lines. In cloudy conditions it closes its wings, but can fly even at low temperatures. The males spend much of their time flying over low vegetation in search of females, stopping off occasionally to drink nectar from moss campion and marsh andromeda. The eggs are laid on cloudberry, bearberry and bog bilberry. The winter is spent as a small caterpillar, which begins to feed the following spring.

A Frejya's Fritillary at rest among mosses and dwarf sallow at the edge of a bog. The butterfly has a low zigzag flight, and spends much of its time basking on bare ground or on mosses and lichens with wings widespread.

WHERE This northern species is widespread in Norway, Sweden and Finland from lowland to 1,000 m.

WHEN Flies from early June until mid-July, but this may vary with climatic conditions.

LOOKALIKES

The zigzag black line across the hindwing distinguishes it from three similar northern fritillaries: the **Arctic** (*Clossiana chariclea*), **Polar** (*C. polaris*) and **Frigga's** (*C. frigga*) fritillaries. These are much more localised and scarce.

Weaver's Fritillary

Boloria (Clossiana) dia

Underside of Weaver's Fritillary, roosting pose. The butterflies roost or rest in bad weather with wings closed and the forewing retracted, showing the sharply angled hindwing.

The fully grown caterpillar is grey-black with pale spines along its body and two longer ones behind the head. It feeds on the leaves of several species of violets.

Weaver's Fritillary 35 mm

Small White 43mm

The chrysalis is bronze-brown with metallic spots on its back, and is suspended from a plant stem.

Weaver's Fritillary inhabits sheltered clearings in light woodland, shrubby fields and roadside verges where there are plentiful wild flowers. It is one of the smallest fritillaries, and is easily distinguished from other species by the shape of its hindwings. The upperside pattern is quite similar to that of the Pearl-bordered Fritillary, but the row of black spots around the outer margin of the wings is often more prominently marked, and in general the black markings tend to be bolder. The butterfly is active, but tends to fly low over vegetation, and rarely flies great distances. It seeks nectar from a wide variety of flowers, especially marjoram, catmint and other plants in the deadnettle family. The eggs are often laid on dead leaves or plant stems as well as violet leaves, and the winter is spent as a part-grown caterpillar.

A male Weaver's Fritillary basks with open wings on a hawkbit flower head. Notice the sharp angle between the leading and outer edges of the hindwings.

WHERE Widespread and often common through a wide swathe of mainland Europe, but absent from southern Spain, southern Italy, Britain and Scandinavia.

WHEN Depending on locality it can complete two or three generations in a year, and adults can be seen from April through to late summer.

LOOKALIKES

The underside hindwing resembles **Titania's Fritillary** (page 146), but has silver-white spots at the centre and around the margins. It flies at lower altitudes than the **Mountain** (page 142) and **Shepherd's** fritillaries (*Boloria pales*).

Dusky-winged Fritillary

Boloria (Clossiana) improba

Underside of the Dusky-winged Fritillary.

Upperside of Little Fritillary (see lookalikes). This species flies only in the Alps, so could not be confused with the Dusky-winged Fritillary in the Arctic.

Egg of Dusky-winged Fritillary.

Dusky-winged Fritillary 33 mm

Small White 43mm

Despite its very narrow geographical range this butterfly can sometimes be abundant where it occurs. It lives on open tundra grasslands, but often in sheltered hollows on hillsides. The dark, obscurely marked wings have a unique and subtle beauty, and give the butterflies excellent camouflage when they settle. They take to the wing infrequently, and, except when engaged in territorial confrontations or courtship, the flight is low, whirring and direct. Once settled they are extremely difficult to locate. Both sexes seek nectar from moss campion, or from the small flowers of mountain heath and bog bilberry, which they access by crawling among the tangled stems and foliage of the shrubs. Little is known about the life cycle, but it is believed that the caterpillars' food plants are sallows, and that they may take two years to develop from egg to adult.

The males are territorial, spending much time basking with outspread wings on bare ground, among mosses and dwarf shrubs. They are difficult to locate unless they fly, and even then the flight is hard to follow.

WHERE Confined to Arctic Norway, Sweden and Finland.

WHEN The flight period depends on weather conditions, but may be from late June to early August.

LOOKALIKES

The only remotely similar species is the **Little Fritillary** (*Melitaea asteria*), but this is a very localised species of the central Alps, never met within the Arctic.

Glanville Fritillary

Melitaea cinxia

Upperside of female. Black lines over orange-brown, and a distinctive row of black spots around the outer part of the hindwing.

Underside of male. Note the small black points in the outer band on the hindwing.

In spring, when development is almost complete, the caterpillars separate. The fully grown caterpillar is spiny and black with tiny white spots and a red-brown head.

The chrysalis is often formed in dense grass tussocks. It is greyish-brown to black, with raised yellow marks on its back.

Glanville
Fritillary
43 mm

Small White
43mm

This is one of the most familiar members of a group of fritillaries which have a regular network of black lines over their orange-brown uppersides. In the Glanville Fritillary there is also a row of black spots on the hindwing. The male forewings are slightly concave on the outer margin, giving them a pointed appearance. The female is yellowish- orange, and often has more extensive black markings. The underside hindwing in both sexes is white with black-edged orange patches and bands, black marks along the outer edge, and a row of black spots in the outer orange band. The butterflies are powerful flyers, but spend much of their time sipping nectar from flowers or basking with open wings. The eggs are laid in large batches on the leaves of plantains or speedwells, and initially the caterpillars feed together on a silken web, in which they also hibernate.

A male Glanville Fritillary basks with open wings. Notice the row of black spots on the hindwing, and the black-and-white chequered fringes. Compound flowers such as scabious, thistles and hawkweeds are favourite nectar sources.

WHERE Common and widespread throughout Europe as far north as southern Scandinavia. In Britain it is mostly confined to the southern coastal strip of the Isle of Wight.

WHEN Usually one generation a year; on the wing from early May through to July. Further south a second brood emerges August to September.

LOOKALIKES

The black spots on the upperside hindwing separate it from similar fritillaries except for **Knapweed Fritillary** (page 156), whose outer orange band on the underside hindwing has a row of reddish spots without black points.

Knapweed Fritillary

Melitaea phoebe

Underside of Knapweed Fritillary. The ground colour of the hindwing underside varies from white to creamy-yellow, with black-bordered orange bands. The outer band is yellowish with reddish central patches.

The fully-grown caterpillar is spiny and grey-black with variable amounts of white spotting. The winter is spent as a part-grown caterpillar.

Knapweed Fritillary
42 mm

The chrysalis is grey-brown with white, yellow and black markings.

Small White
43mm

This is a variable species, in which the black upperside markings are often reduced and incomplete. In some populations, especially those occurring in high, sub-alpine meadows, there is a marked contrast between darker red-brown and paler, yellowish bands on the upperside. The butterfly inhabits dry, open grassland, roadside verges and abandoned agricultural land where the caterpillars' food plants, various knapweeds, grow. It has a swift, graceful flight, and spends much of its time basking with open wings on stones or bare ground, or drinking nectar from thistles, knapweeds and other flowers. It frequently drinks moisture from damp patches on the ground. The eggs are laid in large batches on the caterpillars' food plants. The young caterpillars feed communally on webs, but disperse in their final stage.

A male Knapweed Fritillary perching with open wings on a flower head. Notice the greatly enlarged third orange patch on the margin of the forewing. This specimen lacks black spots on the hindwing (which are present in some specimens).

WHERE The butterfly is widespread and often common in Western, southern and central Europe, but absent from northern Europe, including Britain and Scandinavia.

WHEN Usually two generations in a year, with a spring brood flying from mid-April to mid-June and a summer one flying mostly in July and August.

LOOKALIKES

Well-marked specimens are very similar to the **Glanville Fritillary** (page 154), but on the upperside forewing one of the marginal orange patches is much larger than the rest and interrupts the next row.

Spotted Fritillary

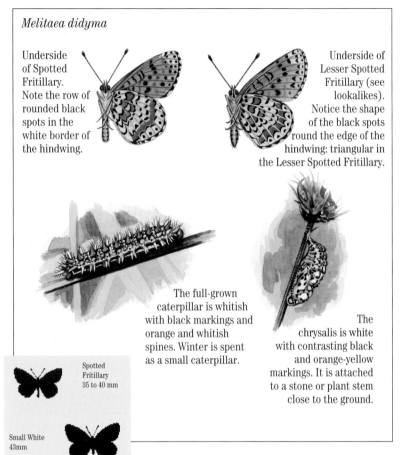

Melitaea didyma

Underside of Spotted Fritillary. Note the row of rounded black spots in the white border of the hindwing.

Underside of Lesser Spotted Fritillary (see lookalikes). Notice the shape of the black spots round the edge of the hindwing: triangular in the Lesser Spotted Fritillary.

The full-grown caterpillar is whitish with black markings and orange and whitish spines. Winter is spent as a small caterpillar.

The chrysalis is white with contrasting black and orange-yellow markings. It is attached to a stone or plant stem close to the ground.

Spotted Fritillary
35 to 40 mm

Small White
43mm

Dry, flowery grassland, Mediterranean scrubland and abandoned agricultural land are favoured habitats. The male upperside is orange-red, and in southern districts it has a brilliant, fiery hue. The black markings are reduced to scattered spots. The female usually has a paler, yellowish-orange upperside, with stronger black markings and often, especially in the south, a suffusion of grey and black scales. The males bask with open wings on prominent perches, and drink nectar from thistles and knapweeds. The females are more sedentary, and bask on rocks or bare ground, or seek out suitable plants on which to lay their eggs. These are placed in batches on the leaves of low-growing plants, especially plantains but also speedwells, foxgloves and others. The resulting caterpillars feed collectively in a web until almost full-grown.

A male Spotted Fritillary basks with open wings in bright sunshine. The brilliant red of the male's upperside, and reduced black markings, distinguish it from all other fritillaries, except for the Lesser Spotted Fritillary.

WHERE Widespread through Western, Central and Southern Europe, but most likely to be seen in the south.

WHEN Depending on locality, there are up to three generations a year, and the butterflies can be seen from April to September.

LOOKALIKES

The black borders of the bands on the underside hindwing are dashed, unlike on the **Knapweed** (page 156) and **Glanville fritillaries** (page 154). The **Lesser Spotted Fritillary** (*Melitaea trivia*) see the paintings opposite.

Heath Fritillary

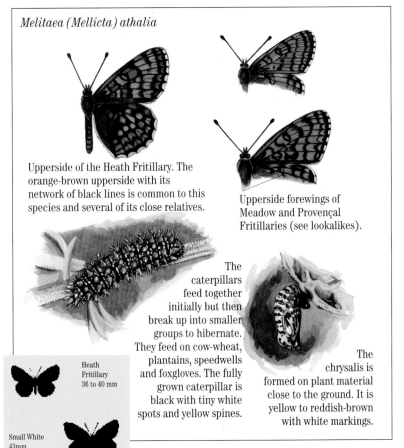

Melitaea (Mellicta) athalia

Upperside of the Heath Fritillary. The orange-brown upperside with its network of black lines is common to this species and several of its close relatives.

Upperside forewings of Meadow and Provençal Fritillaries (see lookalikes).

The caterpillars feed together initially but then break up into smaller groups to hibernate. They feed on cow-wheat, plantains, speedwells and foxgloves. The fully grown caterpillar is black with tiny white spots and yellow spines.

The chrysalis is formed on plant material close to the ground. It is yellow to reddish-brown with white markings.

Heath Fritillary 36 to 40 mm

Small White 43mm

The Heath Fritillary is the most common and widespread of a group of similar fritillaries. The upperside pattern of orange-brown with a fine network of black lines is shared by the group. The undersides, too, are similar, having a continuous network of fine black lines, two orange bands and two fine parallel lines at the hindwing margins. The favoured haunts of the butterfly in the northern part of its range are clearings in coppiced woodland and sheltered areas in heath and moorland. However, a wider range of habitats is used in southern Europe, and it remains quite common there. In woodland, the low-growing plants on which the caterpillars feed are soon shaded out, and the butterflies need to be able to colonize fresh habitats nearby. In Britain and some other countries, changes in woodland management have led to local extinctions.

The underside of a male. Notice the lattice pattern of black lines on the hindwing, and the wide black inner border to the lower orange marginal spots on the forewing. This is a useful feature for distinguishing the Heath Fritillary from some of its lookalikes.

WHERE Common throughout much of Europe, but very localized and threatened in southern England and some other countries in the northern part of its range.

WHEN Usually one generation, emerging over a long period from April on. In some places and seasons a second brood flies in August and September.

LOOKALIKES

Orange marginal spots on the **Meadow Fritillary** forewing (*M. parthenoides*) are very regular (third one larger in the Heath Fritillary). The **Provençal Fritillary** (*M. deione*) may have a dumbbell-shaped mark on the forewing.

False Heath Fritillary

Melitaea diamina

The underside hindwing is quite similar to the Heath Fritillary, but it has dark spots in the outer orange band, and the fine marginal parallel lines are in-filled with yellow.

The young caterpillars feed together and hibernate in a silken web. They disperse and complete their development in spring. They are similar in appearance to the caterpillars of the Heath Fritillary.

The chrysalis is very similar to that of the Spotted Fritillary: white with black and yellow markings.

False Heath Fritillary 35 mm

Small White 43mm

This species inhabits damp flower-rich meadows and marshes as well as wide rides and clearings in woodland. It often flies together with other small fritillaries, but the upperside is quite distinctive as the black markings on the hindwing are very extensive and fused, reducing the orange-brown ground colour to rows of small spots. In some individuals this is also true of the forewings. The female is similar, but the ground colour of her upperside is more yellowish-orange. The black-and-white chequered fringes are quite noticeable. In some parts of southern Europe the upperside is paler and correct identification depends on the underside pattern. The butterflies bask with open wings or feed on flowers in sunshine. The eggs are laid on cow-wheat, plantains, and speedwells.

A male False Heath Fritillary basks on a perch in a wet meadow. The very dark colour of the upperside is distinctive, but confusion can be caused by much paler forms which fly in southern districts. These closely resemble the Heath Fritillary.

WHERE Widespread and sometimes common in western and central Europe, but localised or absent from the far south and northern Scandinavia. Absent from Britain.

WHEN On the wing from May to July in one brood, or two broods in May and June, then August and September, depending on locality.

LOOKALIKES

The darker upperside and black spots on the underside hindwing separate this species from the **Heath Fritillary** (page 160) in most areas.

Lapland Fritillary

Euphydryas (Hypodryas) iduna

Underside of the Lapland Fritillary. The underside pattern is very similar to the upperside, and males are similar to females except that the latter have more rounded forewings.

Upperside of male Cynthia's Fritillary (see lookalikes). Notice the small black spots in the orange band on the hindwing, and the brilliance of the white markings.

The fully grown caterpillar is black, with bristly spines and yellow spots.

The chrysalis is cream with black spots.

Lapland Fritillary 38mm

Small White 43mm

This butterfly belongs to the same group of fritillaries as the Marsh Fritillary, but is the only one that occurs so far north in Europe. The strongly contrasting black-bordered red and whitish bands on the wings are very striking and distinctive. The typical habitat is among mosses, low-growing herbs and dwarf shrubs in open areas around marshes and lakes, but they also inhabit bare, rocky areas at higher altitudes. In sunshine, the males fly rapidly low over the vegetation, in a zigzag flight. They are territorial, and, when settled on a favoured perch, fly up to intercept passing butterflies, even those of other species, as well as potential mates. The eggs are laid in small clusters on speedwells, plantains and *Vaccinium* species, and the resulting caterpillars feed communally.

A male basks among marsh vegetation, with its wings spread wide. In cool, cloudy weather the butterflies close their wings, often hiding in dense vegetation. When the sun comes out they open them again, but take several minutes to warm up enough to fly.

WHERE In Europe this butterfly is confined to Arctic Norway, Sweden and Finland, but is quite widespread and often common within its restricted range.

WHEN The flight period is short, and variable according to the weather conditions: usually between mid-June and late July.

LOOKALIKES

Male **Cynthia's Fritillaries** (*E. cynthia*) are similar, but their hindwing marks set them apart - see painting opposite. There is no overlap in their geographical distribution, so confusion is unlikely.

Marsh Fritillary

Euphydryas aurinia

Underside of the Marsh Fritillary. Note the black spots in the outer orange band on the hindwing.

Upperside of the Asian Fritillary (see lookalikes). This Alpine species lacks spots in the orange band on the hindwing.

The fully grown caterpillar is spiny and black with minute white freckles that concentrate to form bands along the sides.

The chrysalis is pale bluish-white with black and orange-yellow markings, and is formed among vegetation close to the ground.

Marsh Fritillary 40mm

Small White 43mm

Marsh Fritillaries live in scattered colonies, each of which may be very limited in area. They inhabit flowery grassland habitats, sometimes wet meadows or marshland, but also chalk downland and dry, coastal cliffs. Many colonies are greatly threatened by agricultural intensification. In central and northern Europe the favoured food plant for the caterpillar is devil's-bit scabious, but other scabious species, honeysuckles and gentians may be used. The males fly low, searching for females, which are less active, and rest low down in vegetation. The eggs are laid in large batches, up to 300 or more, on the undersides of scabious leaves. The young caterpillars feed in large groups, within a silken web. They spend the winter in the web, but in spring complete their growth separately. A very small form occurs in mountains (*f. debilis*).

A male rests on valerian. There are numerous named variant forms of the Marsh Fritillary. This is f. provincialis, which flies in southern France. The yellow and orange bands, combined with black spots in the orange band on the hindwing, are distinctive.

WHERE Widely distributed throughout Europe, but local in Britain and southern Scandinavia, and threatened in many areas by agricultural change.

WHEN Adults are on the wing from mid April or later, depending on locality and altitude.

LOOKALIKES

Asian (*E. intermedia*) and **Cynthia's** (*E. cynthia*) fritillaries are confined to the Alps. The **Scarce Fritillary** (*H. maturna*) is now very rare; the **Spanish Fritillary** (*E. desfontainii*) occurs in Iberia and north Africa.

Marbled White/Western Marbled White

Marbled White
Melanargia galathea

Western Marbled White
M. occitancia

Upperside of Marbled White. The bold black-and-white 'chessboard' pattern is distinctive.

The upperside of the Western Marbled White has a subtler pattern of black spots and striations on its white ground colour. The black spots are often blue-centred.

The caterpillar of the marbled white is plain green or brown, with darker lines along its back and sides.

The chrysalis of the Marbled White is whitish on the on the underside, shading to yellow and is formed among leaf litter.

Marbled White
45-50 mm
Western
Marbled White
45-50 mm

Small White
43mm

There are several species of **Marbled White** in Europe. Despite their mainly white colouration, they belong to the group of 'brown' butterflies (see introduction, p. 17). The Marbled White inhabits tall, often tussocky grassland, but the young larvae also require fine grasses, and the adults take nectar from grassland flowers such as scabious and thistles. The winter is spent as a small caterpillar.

The **Western Marbled White** lives in hot, dry, sparsely vegetated and often rocky areas, with *Brachypodium*, *Festuca* and other grasses. The eggs are laid singly on the grasses, and the resulting small caterpillars rest through the summer, only feeding during winter and early spring. They are similar in appearance to the caterpillars of the Marbled White.

Underside of a male **Marbled White**, *feeding from bramble. In some specimens the underside hindwing is plain white.*

Underside of **Western Marbled White**: *the beautiful brown outlining of the wing veins is distinctive.*

WHERE AND WHEN
The Marbled White is widespread and often common throughout Europe except Scandinavia, northern Britain and most of Iberia. It flies in June and July in one brood.

Marbled White

Western Marbled White

WHERE AND WHEN
The Western Marbled White occurs in southern France, Spain and Portugal. It flies from late April to June.

Woodland Grayling

Hipparchia fagi

Underside of male. The hindwing is white, shading to pale brown, covered by a dense network of fine grey-black lines, and two thicker black zigzag lines running across the wing.

The fine black markings are more evenly distributed in the female. In both sexes the ground colour of the underside forewing is dark brown.

The caterpillar is pale fawn, with slightly darker bands along its sides, and a discontinuous darker band along its back. It feeds on various grasses, and hibernates when part-grown.

The chrysalis is fawn shading to red-brown and formed in a loose cell in the earth.

Woodland Grayling
53 mm

Small White
43mm

Woodland Graylings inhabit clearings and open tracks in dry woodland, where they spend much of their time settled on the ground or on tree trunks. When settled with their wings closed, and the forewings lowered between the hindwings, their camouflage is almost perfect. The whitish area in the outer part of the hindwing (see above) is reduced in the female, giving a more uniform appearance to the underside. When disturbed they have a swift, low flight but soon settle again. They are most common at low altitudes, but can be found up to 1,000 m or more. The dark chocolate-brown upperside, with pale whitish to yellow bands, is usually only seen when the butterfly takes to the wing. In the males, the pale band on the forewing is obscured by brown scales.

The upperside of a female. The species always rests with wings closed, but the females open their wings briefly during courtship.

WHERE Widespread in southern and central Europe, but absent from Iberia and from most of northern Europe including Britain and Scandinavia.

WHEN One generation in a year, but the flight period is prolonged: from June to September.

LOOKALIKES

The **Rock Grayling** (*Hipparchia alcyone*) is usually smaller, and flies at higher altitudes, but is difficult to tell apart in the field. The ground colour of the **Grayling's** underside forewings is orange (page 172). See also **Great Banded Grayling**, page 184.

Grayling

Hipparchia semele

Upperside of male Grayling. In males the pale bands around the wing margins are obscured, and there is a dark band on the forewings.

The underside of a female Grayling. Notice the more even distribution of grey-black markings than occurs in the male.

The caterpillar feeds on various grass species, and the winter is spent in this stage. It is grey-brown with darker stripes along its back and sides.

Grayling 50-58 mm

Small White 43mm

The chrysalis is formed in a loose silk web, on or just under the surface of the soil. It is orange-brown with darker wing covers.

The Grayling is the most widespread of this group of butterflies, but it is declining rapidly in some countries as a result of development pressures and agricultural intensification. It inhabits a wide variety of grassland types, but all are dry and well-drained, with sparse vegetation and areas of bare ground. The males are territorial, settling on the ground with wings closed, and flying up to intercept intruders, or chase passing females. They typically settle in hot sun spots on bare ground, edge-on to the sun. They are well camouflaged and often only noticed when they fly up. The males have a dark band of scent scales on the forewings, and the antennae of the female are drawn over these during courtship. The uppersides of the females are more brightly coloured, with yellow-orange bands around the margins.

Male Grayling drinking nectar from lavender. Note the orange underside of the forewing. Graylings often drink moisture from puddles and tree sap, but, as this photo shows, do sometimes visit flowers.

WHERE Widespread throughout Europe, but absent from northern Scandinavia.

WHEN Just one generation in a year, with the adults flying from June to September, depending on season and locality.

LOOKALIKES

The underside forewing ground colour is dark brown in the **Woodland** (page 170) and **Rock** graylings (*Hipparchia alcyone*). There are several other grayling species in Europe, but they cannot be distinguished with certainty in the field.

Tree Grayling

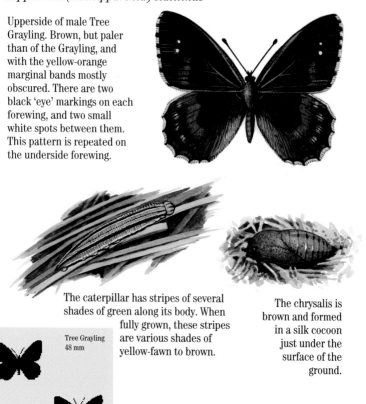

Hipparchia (Neohipparchia) statilinus

Upside of male Tree Grayling. Brown, but paler than of the Grayling, and with the yellow-orange marginal bands mostly obscured. There are two black 'eye' markings on each forewing, and two small white spots between them. This pattern is repeated on the underside forewing.

The caterpillar has stripes of several shades of green along its body. When fully grown, these stripes are various shades of yellow-fawn to brown.

The chrysalis is brown and formed in a silk cocoon just under the surface of the ground.

Tree Grayling
48 mm

Small White
43mm

This species inhabits hot, dry grassy or rocky habitats, sometimes in light woodland, but usually with scattered shrubs. During the hottest part of the day it takes shelter from the sun, often in the shade of a bush, or on a tree trunk, but is more active in the morning and late afternoon. The butterflies are attracted to the flowers of eryngo, scabious and thistles. When settled they almost always keep their wings closed and are extremely well camouflaged, as the irregular markings disguise the wing shape. The patterns on the underside are quite variable from one locality to another. This may be an adaptation to improve camouflage against different background environments. The white eggs are laid singly on grass blades, and the resulting tiny caterpillars hibernate through the winter. They begin feeding on grasses the following spring.

A resting, well-marked male.. Notice how well its colour pattern matches the dappled light and shade of the rock, and the lichens. The females are similar, but usually with less contrasty colour patterns, and with the wavy lines across the hindwing obscure or absent.

WHERE Fairly widespread in southern and western Europe, but absent from the north, including Scandinavia and Britain.

WHEN One generation a year, with adults flying in July, August, and September, or later in some districts.

LOOKALIKES

Freyer's Grayling (*H fatua*) is similar, but larger, and in Europe confined to Greece and the Balkans.

Striped Grayling

Hipparchia fidia

Upperside of male Striped Grayling: dark grey-brown with two black eye spots in each forewing, and two white spots between them. The paler bands in the outer part of the wings are mostly obscured, and the white fringes are chequered with black.

The caterpillar rests until autumn, but may continue to feed in the winter, completing its development in the spring. It is pale green with darker stripes along its body in its early stages, but is brown-striped when fully grown.

Striped Grayling
48 mm

Small White
43mm

This butterfly inhabits hot, dry areas, usually with bare, rocky outcrops among grasses and shrubs or light woodland. It spends most of its time at rest on the rocks with its wings closed. Under normal conditions one only sees the underside, and this is most distinctive. The ground colour is silver-grey to greyish-brown, with black zigzag lines, a white band across both wings, and large, yellow-ringed 'eye' spots on the forewing.The butterflies remain motionless on the rocks for considerable periods, but fly up and exchange places from time to time. When they do so the flight is usually short and fast. Courtship and mating take place on and around their resting places. The winter is spent as a caterpillar, and the chrysalis is formed close to the ground among leaf litter.

A mating pair of Striped Graylings settle on a rocky slope in full sun. Note the matching colours of their wings and the surrounding rocks and lichens. The 'eye' markings on the forewings tend to be revealed only when the butterflies are alarmed, or about to fly.

WHERE A south-western distribution in Europe: southern France, north-west Italy and Iberia.

WHEN One generation a year, with adults flying from the end of June through to October.

LOOKALIKES

No other European grayling has black zigzag markings on the underside hindwing.

Hermit

Hipparchia (Chazara) briseis

Underside of female Hermit: note the small size of the 'eye' spot on the forewing (see lookalikes).

Upperside of a male Hermit. Note the pale yellowish bands across both wings, broken by darker edging to the veins in the forewing.

The winter is spent as a small caterpillar, which begins feeding on grasses in the spring. The fully grown caterpillar has interrupted dark grey stripes along its back and sides.

The chrysalis is smooth and brown, shading to yellowish (similar to that of the Tree Grayling). It is formed in a cell just below the surface of the soil.

Hermit
55-60 mm

Small White
43mm

The Hermit lives in hot, dry grassland and rocky slopes. It is threatened in some areas by the cessation of sheep grazing and the consequent shading out of its habitat by the growth of shrubs and trees. When settled on rocks, the male is superbly camouflaged. The pale fawn ground colour of the underside, shading to brown, with bold blocks of darker brown, breaks up the outline of the butterfly, and matches fissures and hollows in the rocks. The underside of the female has a more evenly coloured hindwing, but the forewing is similar. Like most other graylings, the upperside is only seen when the butterfly is in flight. The female is usually larger than the male, and the pale bands are usually white. There is a minority form in which the bands are brownish.

*A male Hermit drinks nectar from a pink (*Dianthus*)
growing in hot, sparse grassland. Hermits also visit
thistles, scabious and other flowers, but are more often
seen at rest on rocks and bare ground.*

WHERE Widespread through central
and southern Europe, but is absent
from Britain and northern Europe.

WHEN One generation in a year, with
the butterflies on the wing from June
to September.

LOOKALIKES

The male underside pattern is
distinctive. The female could be
confused with a poorly marked
female **Tree Grayling** (page 174),
but the latter has much larger
'eye' spots on the forewing
undersides.

Great Sooty Satyr

Hipparchia (Satyrus) ferula

Upside of male Great Sooty Satyr. The males are very dark – with two small white-centered 'eye' spots on each forewing.

Underside of male Great Sooty Satyr. The underside hindwing is densely marked with dark brown and black cross lines, with a paler band in the outer part of the wing.

Underside of female Great Sooty Satyr is usually much paler than the male's.

Upside of male Black Satyr (see lookalikes). It has only one 'eye' spot on the forewing.

The fully grown caterpillar is cream-white with darker grey/ black bands along its back and sides. It feeds mainly on sheep's fescue grass. The winter is spent in this stage.

Great Sooty Satyr 55 mm

Small White 43mm

The Great Sooty Satyr occurs on hot, dry slopes with sparse vegetation and exposed bare ground and rocks, but at low altitudes can also be found in open areas in light woodland and scrub. Both sexes feed actively from thistles, knapweeds, lavender and other flowers, often with wings part-open. The female (see photograph opposite) is paler on the upperside, with larger 'eye' spots. In both sexes there are often small white spots between the 'eye' spots. Males patrol grassy slopes in search of the females, which fly less frequently. Both sexes bask with open wings in late afternoon sunshine. In some lights the wings of the males show a metallic reflection. Both sexes have prominent 'eye' spots near the tips of the underside forewings. The chrysalis is formed on the ground among leaf-litter.

A female Great Sooty Satyr basks on a rock with wide open wings. Unlike most of the graylings, this species can often be seen with open wings, especially in early morning sunshine and late in the afternoon. Note the two large 'eye' spots on each forewing.

WHERE Widespread and often common in suitable habitat in southern and south-western Europe, but absent from most of Spain.

WHEN One generation in a year, with butterflies on the wing from June though July and into August.

LOOKALIKES

The **Black Satyr** (*H. actaea*) has just one 'eye' spot on each forewing. The **Dryad** has blue 'pupils' in its 'eye' spots (see page 182).

Dryad

Hipparchia (Minois) dryas

Upperside of female. The blue-centred 'eye' spots are usually larger in the females.

Upperside of male. Both sexes are very dark brown, the males almost black.

The caterpillar is pale grey with darker continuous stripes along its sides, and a broken one along its back. It feeds on grasses and possibly sedges.

The chrysalis is brown, shading to orange, and is formed among leaf litter in grass tussocks.

Dryad
48-60 mm

Small White
43mm

The Dryad lives in tall, flowery grassland, usually with bushes, or at the edge of woodland. It also inhabits wetlands at the edge of lakes or streams, usually in lowlands or at medium altitudes in mountainous areas. The large size, slow, flapping flight, and very dark brown colour are distinctive. The underside of the male is dark brown with 'eye' spots on the forewing narrowly ringed with orange. The female underside is much paler, with contrasting bands on the hindwing. Both sexes are attracted to flowers, especially scabious. In lowland sites they are often threatened by agricultural intensification, where grassland is converted to arable, or heavily grazed. They are surprisingly difficult to approach for photography. The winter is spent as a young caterpillar.

A male settles with wings closed among dense grasses. Notice the scalloped hindwing edge. They bask with open wings in sunshine. Their flight is low and seems slow and lazy, but they are surprisingly difficult to follow as they disappear behind a bush or hedge.

WHERE Widespread but localised through southern, central and eastern Europe. Absent from most of Spain and northern Europe.

WHEN On the wing in July and August, in one generation.

LOOKALIKES

The males of the **Great Sooty** (page 180) and **Black Satyrs** (*H. actaea*) are similar to the Dryad, but their 'eye' spots are brilliant white (pale blue in the Dryad). Note, also, the scalloped edge to the hindwing in the Dryad.

Great Banded Grayling

Hipparchia (Kanetisa) circe

Upperside of male. In both sexes the upperside is very dark brown to black, with a pale band across both fore- and hindwings. This is broken on the forewings, with a small 'eye' spot.

The chrysalis is orange-brown, and is formed in a loose cell made of silk threads and soil particles.

The fully grown caterpillar is grey with continuous darker bands along its back and sides. The winter is spent as a part-grown caterpillar, and, like other graylings, the food plants are various species of grass.

Great Banded Grayling 63 mm

Small White 43mm

This species favours sunny, dry grassland with shrubs, and open woodland, from sea level to medium altitudes. It spends much of its time settled on rocks, tree trunks or bare ground, tracks and paths, and is especially well camouflaged at rest on a tree trunk. Usually it rests with its wings closed. The flight is swift and acrobatic. This and the strongly contrasting uppersides are reminiscent of the White Admirals. However, as soon as this species settles the underside pattern is seen to be different (see page 118). In very hot places the species rests through the hottest part of the summer, and reappears in late August. At this time of the year they are often seen drinking nectar from thistle flowers, when they sometimes flick open their wings for a few seconds.

A Great Banded Grayling settles on a rock face. Notice the prominent white band on the hindwing and, closer to the body, another partial white band. This helps to separate this species from other similar graylings.

WHERE Widespread and often common throughout central and southern Europe.

WHEN One prolonged flight period, from June through to September.

LOOKALIKES

The undersides of the **White Admirals** are very different (see page 118). The **Woodland** (page 170) and **Rock Graylings** (*H. alcyone*) are usually smaller and have only one white band on the underside hindwing.

False Grayling

Hipparchia (Arethusana) arethusa

Upperside of False Grayling. Notice the chequered fringes.

The fully grown caterpillar is pale fawn-brown, with darker stripes along its back and sides, the one on the back narrower than those on the sides. The winter is spent as a small caterpillar, and in spring it completes its development, feeding on various grass species.

The chrysalis is smooth and orange-brown, formed within a grass tussock.

False Grayling 40-45 mm

Small White 43mm

This species, like most of the grayling group, is a sun-lover. However, it is distinctive in spending much of its time drinking nectar from flowers, such as *eryngo*, scabious and thyme. It favours warm, grassy hillsides, or open areas in woodland and scrub, with plenty of flowers. When it feeds it does so with its wings closed, and makes only brief flights between flower heads. The underside hindwing is very variable in colouration, often with marked bands of lighter and darker brown and with an ill-defined whitish band. In some forms the hindwing is more uniformly brown, and the females are usually paler and less strongly marked on the underside. The bright orange bands on the upperside (both sexes) are broken by dark scaling along the veins.

A male drinks nectar from a flower head of eryngo.
Note the orange ground colour of the forewing, and the
gently curved wavy line across the hindwing. This
specimen has the veins on the hindwing narrowly
outlined in white, which is useful for identification.

WHERE Discontinuous distribution in Europe. It is widespread in Western and South-western Europe and also occurs in Eastern Europe, Greece and the Balkans.

WHEN Flies in one generation from mid June through to mid September, but is most common in August.

LOOKALIKES

The **Grayling** (page 172) is usually larger, and the line running across the middle of the underside is sharply irregular, as opposed to more smoothly wavy in the False Grayling.

Norse Grayling

Oeneis norna

Upperside of male Norse Grayling. Usually pale brown with a variable number of small 'eye' spots.

Underside of the Alpine Grayling. This lacks a clearly marked darker band across the hindwing. Its range does not overlap with that of the Norse Grayling (see lookalikes).

The underside of the Arctic Grayling has a more evenly curved band on the hindwing and usually lacks an 'eye' spot on the forewing (see lookalikes).

Norse Grayling 45 mm

Small White 43mm

The favoured haunts of this butterfly are at the edges of bogs, marshy clearings among dwarf birches or along the margins of streams, up to 900 m in altitude. They open their wings very briefly when they settle, but usually rest and roost with them closed, either on the ground or on the bark of birch trees. The males appear to be territorial, often pursuing females and also intruders of other species. On the underside hindwing there is an irregular dark band, edged with white in the male. The males also have a dark band of scent scales on the upperside. It is very closely related to the Alpine Grayling (see lookalikes, opposite), which is confined to the Alps. The caterpillars feed on grasses and take two years to develop. They are yellow with brown stripes on their backs and sides.

A male Norse Grayling settled but alert among low-growing vegetation in a boggy forest clearing, northern Sweden. The butterflies are fast-flying and difficult to approach once disturbed. However, in cool, overcast conditions they become torpid.

WHERE This northern species is widespread but quite local through Norway, Sweden and Finland.

WHEN The adults can be seen in June or July, depending on the season.

LOOKALIKES

The **Alpine Grayling** (*Oeneis glacialis*) occurs only in the Alps. The **Arctic Grayling** (*O. bore*) flies in the north and is very similar. The patterning on the underside hindwings is variable, but a useful way of telling the species apart.

Arran Brown

Erebia ligea

Underside of male Arran Brown. Notice the white mark on the hindwing. The female's underside is usually paler and more variegated, but it also has a distinctive white band across the hindwing.

Underside of male Large Ringlet.

Arran Brown
45 mm

Small White
43mm

Upperside of Large Ringlet (see lookalikes). The black 'eye' spots often lack white 'pupils' usually present in Arran Brown.

This is one of a very large group of brown ringlet butterflies (genus *Erebia*). Unfortunately only a few of this fascinating group can be shown here and on the following pages. Like most of the ringlets, the Arran Brown is typically a mountain butterfly, but it does not fly at the higher altitudes, and is considered a lowland species in Scandinavia. It favours tall, flowery grassland, open tracks and clearings in forests, often close to water. It is one of the largest of the *Erebia* group, and one of the most brightly coloured, the orange bands on the upperside contrasting strongly with the dark brown ground colour. The butterflies spend much of their time drinking nectar from scabious, thistles and other flowers. The males also drink from wet patches on bare ground and tracks.

A female drinks nectar from scabious, with wings widespread. Notice the black-and-white chequered wing fringes. These, and the brightly contrasting orange and brown upperside plus the well-marked, white-pupilled 'eye' spots, help to identify this species.

WHERE A discontinuous distribution in Europe. Widespread in hilly and mountainous areas of central and southern Europe and also throughout most of Norway, Sweden, Finland and the Baltic, mainly as a lowland species.

WHEN One generation in a year, on the wing during July and August.

LOOKALIKES

The chequered wing fringes separate it from most other ringlets. The white mark or band on the underside hindwing separates it from the very similar **Large Ringlet** (*Erebia euryale*) (see the paintings opposite).

Scotch Argus

Erebia aethiops

The male underside is distinctive, with tiny white spots in a silver-grey band on the hindwing.

Underside of female Scotch Argus. Paler, with a dark band, and tiny white spots on the hindwing.

When fully grown it is pale brown with darker stripes of varying width and is clothed with short dark green or brown-tipped hairs.

The chrysalis is pale brown with fine darker markings. It is formed in a loose web in leaf litter close to the ground.

Scotch Argus 40 mm

Small White 43mm

The Scotch Argus inhabits sparsely vegetated grassy and rocky slopes at low to medium altitudes in mountains, moorland, clearings in woodland and scrub, as well as coastal grasslands and dunes, especially in the north. The upperside is similar to several other medium- to large-sized ringlets, but the underside is distinctive. This has a row of three or four tiny white spots. The males drink fluid from damp ground, but both sexes frequently visit flowers such as thistles, scabious and knapweeds. When searching for females, the males fly low among tussocks of grass, investigating dead leaves or other brown objects. The eggs are laid among tall grasses, and the winter is spent as a small caterpillar. The caterpillars feed on grasses the following spring.

A female Scotch Argus basking with open wings on heather. Notice the dark brown to black ground colour and orange-red bands with white-centred 'eye' spots. The smaller spot in the forewing band is sometimes absent.

WHERE Mainly in central and south-eastern Europe, but also widespread in suitable habitats in northern Britain.

WHEN One prolonged flight period, from July to September.

LOOKALIKES

The tiny white points and absence of an orange band on the underside hindwing are distinctive.

Mountain Ringlet/Lesser Mountain Ringlet

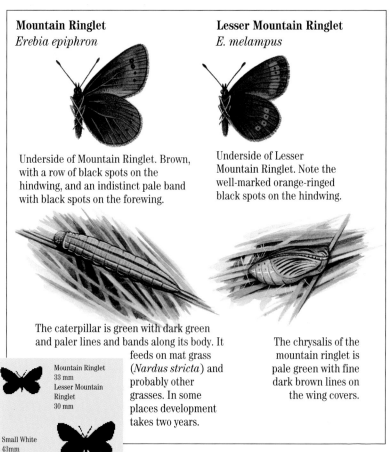

Mountain Ringlet
Erebia epiphron

Lesser Mountain Ringlet
E. melampus

Underside of Mountain Ringlet. Brown, with a row of black spots on the hindwing, and an indistinct pale band with black spots on the forewing.

Underside of Lesser Mountain Ringlet. Note the well-marked orange-ringed black spots on the hindwing.

The caterpillar is green with dark green and paler lines and bands along its body. It feeds on mat grass (*Nardus stricta*) and probably other grasses. In some places development takes two years.

The chrysalis of the mountain ringlet is pale green with fine dark brown lines on the wing covers.

Mountain Ringlet 33 mm
Lesser Mountain Ringlet 30 mm

Small White 43mm

The **Mountain Ringlet** favours open grassland on mountain slopes, often associated with wetter areas, gullies, or grassy clearings amongst shrubs. They bask in the sun with open wings, but disappear into deep vegetation in cold or wet weather. The upperside is medium brown, with an irregular row of black spots in the orange marginal band. There are numerous named local forms of this variable species.

The **Lesser Mountain Ringlet** is very similar, but the orange band and black spots on the upperside are more regular. The brown ground colour of the males is very dark, contrasting with the red-orange marginal bands. They frequently visit flowers, especially yellow members of the dandelion family, on which they bask with open wings in sunshine. The caterpillar hibernates when part-grown. The chrysalis is whitish with black markings.

A female **Mountain Ringlet** *basking with open wings. The wing pattern is less strongly contrasting than that of the Lesser Mountain Ringlet.*

A male **Lesser Mountain Ringlet,** *also basking with open wings. Notice the more even width of the broken orange band on the forewing of the Lesser Mountain Ringlet.*

WHERE AND WHEN
The Mountain Ringlet is widespread in mountains in Europe, including northern Britain, and flies from June to August.

Mountain Ringlet

Lesser Mountain Ringlet

WHERE AND WHEN
The Lesser Mountain Ringlet is confined to the Alps in Europe, but is often very common. It flies from July to September.

Arctic Ringlet

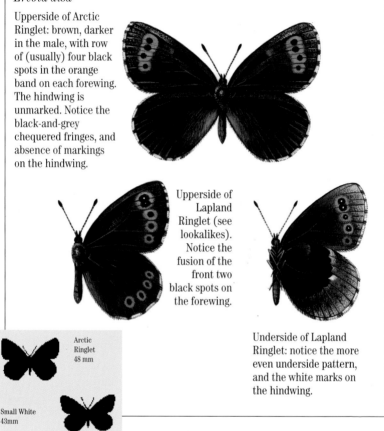

Erebia disa

Upperside of Arctic Ringlet: brown, darker in the male, with row of (usually) four black spots in the orange band on each forewing. The hindwing is unmarked. Notice the black-and-grey chequered fringes, and absence of markings on the hindwing.

Upperside of Lapland Ringlet (see lookalikes). Notice the fusion of the front two black spots on the forewing.

Arctic Ringlet 48 mm

Small White 43mm

Underside of Lapland Ringlet: notice the more even underside pattern, and the white marks on the hindwing.

The Arctic Ringlet is rather localized even within its restricted northern range. However, it can often be common in its favoured localities, which are open mossy and grassy marshes and bogs at 350 m or higher, often with extensive areas of standing water. Its flight is low, and seems weak and fluttering. It frequents rushes and sedges at the edge of marshes, but it also flies along woodland edges and among bushes. It takes wing only in sunshine, and disappears into deep vegetation in cold and cloudy conditions. The underside hindwing is brown, but with a partial dusting of white scales that leaves a wavy-edged darker brown band across the wing, and, often, an additional indistinct dark brown line. Males begin to fly early in the morning, in search of females.

A female Arctic Ringlet settles among low-growing vegetation at the edge of a bog. Notice the well-marked dark band across the hindwing, and absence of black or orange marginal spots or bands. When disturbed, they fly only a short distance, but are hard to locate.

WHERE Rather localised in northern Finland and Scandinavia, but often common.

WHEN The flight period varies according to the weather, but is usually from late June through July.

LOOKALIKES

The lack of spots on the underside hindwing distinguishes this from the **Large** (*E. euryale*) and **Arctic Woodland** (*E. polaris*) ringlets. **Lapland Ringlet** (*E. embla*) is similar (see painting opposite). See also **Dewy Ringlet** (page 214).

197

Woodland Ringlet

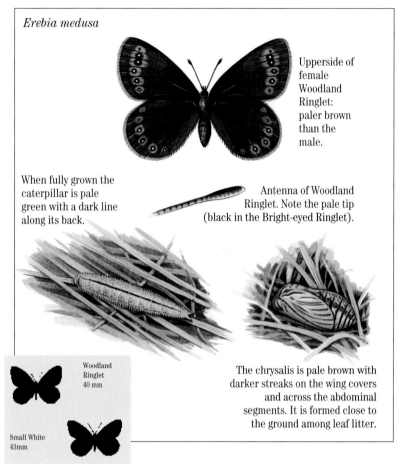

Erebia medusa

Upperside of female Woodland Ringlet: paler brown than the male.

When fully grown the caterpillar is pale green with a dark line along its back.

Antenna of Woodland Ringlet. Note the pale tip (black in the Bright-eyed Ringlet).

The chrysalis is pale brown with darker streaks on the wing covers and across the abdominal segments. It is formed close to the ground among leaf litter.

Woodland Ringlet 40 mm

Small White 43mm

The Woodland Ringlet flies in woodland glades, tracks and edges, where there is dappled sunlight and an abundance of grasses and flowers. It is seen at lower altitudes than most of the ringlets (down to 300 m), but also occurs at high altitudes on more open grassy slopes. The flight appears weak and the butterflies often stop to bask with open wings or drink nectar from flowers. When at rest they are easily approached for photography. The males are very dark brown, and the broken orange bands are less extensive than in the females, but brighter. The pattern on the upperside is repeated on the underside. The wing fringes are uniformly dark brown. The caterpillar feeds on grasses - brome, fescue and others. In some habitats it takes two years to complete its development.

A male Woodland Ringlet settles among tall grasses. Notice the even, dark brown colour pattern, broken by the orange band with 'eye' spots on the forewing and orange-ringed 'eye' spots on the hindwing.

WHERE Widespread and often common in central, eastern and south-eastern Europe, but is absent from the north and south-west.

WHEN Its flight period begins earlier than that of most ringlets, in May, but may be later at higher altitudes. It may be seen until July, or even August.

LOOKALIKES

There are several similar medium-large ringlets. Note absence of chequering of wing fringes, and identical patterns on the underside and upperside. The **Bright-eyed Ringlet** (page 210) has black tips to the underside of the antennae.

Yellow-spotted Ringlet

Erebia manto

Upperside of male. Similar to the Mountain Ringlets, but usually with at most two or three small black spots in the forewing orange band.

Underside of male. Note the spotless orange patches on the hindwing.

The caterpillar is pale yellowish-green with darker stripes along its back and sides, and is clothed in short, dark hairs. It feeds on fescue and other grasses, and takes two years to become fully grown.

The chrysalis is pale yellow-brown with bold dark brown stripes on the wing covers.

Yellow-spotted Ringlet 38 mm

Small White 43mm

The Yellow-spotted Ringlet, like many other ringlet species, is very variable – both individually and from one locality to another. The pattern shown in the photograph is distinctive, but unfortunately not always present. At high altitudes the yellow/orange markings are often much reduced, and in the Pyrenees there is a form (*constans*) in which the males are plain black-brown on both sides. Even here, though, the females usually have some yellow patches on the underside. This species favours lightly grazed upland pastures, sheltered gullies and meadows where there is an abundance of flowers, from 1,000 m to 2,500 m. The flight is rather lazy, and the butterflies spend much of their time drinking nectar from compound flower heads such as thistles, scabious and yellow flowers in the dandelion family. They sunbathe with wings open, often using a flower as a perch.

A female of the typical form of the Yellow-spotted Ringlet drinks with closed wings from a flower. Notice the broken wide yellow band, without spots, on the hindwing. In the male this is more orange-red. No other ringlet has this pattern on the underside.

WHERE Widespread in the Alps and Pyrenees, but it also occurs locally on other European mountain ranges.

WHEN Main flight period is July and August, but varies according to locality and weather.

LOOKALIKES

When the spotless yellow or orange patches are present on the underside hindwing, they are distinctive.

Spring Ringlet

Erebia epistygne

Underside of a male Spring Ringlet. The hindwing is darker than that of the female, and the pale band on the forewing is a deeper shade of orange-red.

Underside of female. Note the whitish outlining of the veins on the hindwing.

Spring Ringlet 45mm

Small White 43mm

The caterpillar is pale brown with darker lines along the back and sides, and a discontinuous whitish band along its sides.

This is one of the larger members of the mountain ringlet group. It has a full complement of white-centred black spots round the wing margins. These are set within a wide, pale band, yellow on the forewings, shading to orange on the hindwings. There is a variable flash of yellow near the middle of the forewings. The Spring Ringlet inhabits rough, tussocky grassland slopes on mountains, often with scattered trees and shrubs. The caterpillars feed on fescue grass in early spring, but then rest until autumn or winter, when the grass is again in suitable condition. The very early flight period of the butterfly is thought to be an adaptation to its dry, southern habitats. The species has become increasingly localised, but can still be quite common where it occurs. The butterflies spend much of their time basking with wings open when the sun shines.

This female was photographed at the beginning of April in the foothills of Mont Ventoux. The males are usually a little darker. They fly only in sunshine, and disappear into deep vegetation when disturbed, or when it clouds over.

WHERE Flies at moderate altitudes in mountains in southern France and eastern Spain.

WHEN It has an exceptionally early flight period, from March through April and into May.

LOOKALIKES

The pattern of spots on the upperside is quite similar to de **Prunner's Ringlet** (*Erebia triaria*) which also flies early. However, the Spring Ringlet's very pale bands and yellow markings in the middle of the forewings are distinctive.

Common Brassy Ringlet

Erebia cassioides

Underside of male Common Brassy Ringlet. Note the silver-grey hindwing.

Upperside of Spanish Brassy Ringlet (*E. hispania*). This species flies in the Pyrenees, and elsewhere in Spain. The 'eye' spots in the forewing are larger than those of the Brassy Ringlet, and the orange surround is more extensive.

The chrysalis is orange-brown to pale green and unmarked.

The caterpillar may be green or beige-brown, with darker longitudinal stripes and paler bands along the sides. It feeds on fescue grasses. The winter is spent as a small caterpillar.

Brassy Ringlet 31 mm

Small White 43mm

The Common Brassy Ringlet is the most widespread of a group of six similar butterflies that occur on the European mountain ranges. They have a distinctive metallic sheen on the upperside, most evident in the males. The upperside is dark brown, a little paler in the females, with two white-centred 'eye' spots on each forewing and three more on the hindwings. They inhabit steep mountain slopes, often in damp areas with lush vegetation. They take nectar from flowers such as thyme, thistles and scabious, and drink moisture from damp patches of bare ground or the edges of mountain tracks. They also often bask with open wings in the sun. The flight of the Brassy Ringlets is very distinctive. The wingbeat is slow, giving them a 'looping', undulating motion low over vegetation. The flight appears weak but can be sustained for long periods.

A male Common Brassy Ringlet is basking in sunlight on bare rock. The brassy reflections are just visible. The butterfly has a distinctive undulating flight, and the undersides flash silver with each wing stroke.

WHERE A scattered distribution in the western and eastern Alps, Pyrenees, Cantabrian mountains, the Massif Central, Appenines and some of the eastern European ranges. They fly at altitudes from 1,500 to 2,500 m.

WHEN Most likely to be seen in July and August.

LOOKALIKES

The brassy reflections distinguish it from all but the other five brassy ringlets. These differ mainly in the size and arrangement of the 'eye' spots on the upperside, but they are often difficult to distinguish in the field.

Water Ringlet

Erebia pronoe

Upperside of male Water Ringlet. The small 'eye' spots are usually enclosed in a small reddish patch, but this is virtually absent in some forms.

The underside of male Marbled Ringlet. Note the white edging of the veins on the hindwing.

Water Ringlet 46 mm

Small White 43mm

The caterpillar is beige-brown with darker bands and lines along its back and sides. It feeds on grasses, mainly fescues.

The chrysalis is orange-brown to pale green and unmarked.

The Water Ringlet inhabits woodland glades and open grassy slopes in mountains, almost always close to streams. It basks and sips fluid from rocks by the water's edge, and sips nectar from flowers growing in damp places: most especially scabious and knapweeds. The male upperside is very dark brown, with two white-centred 'eye' spots on each forewing, enclosed in reddish patches. The underside of the male is very distinctive, the hindwing being silver-grey, with tiny black flecks that are more dense in a band across the middle of the wing. The female underside is paler and more strongly contrasting in its pattern. Her upperside, too, is paler than that of the male, with   larger 'eye' spots and more extensive orange patches. The winter is spent as a small caterpillar.

This male Water Ringlet is sipping liquid from damp earth among rocks by a stream. Note the fine, reflective mottling and lack of prominent 'eye' spots on the hindwing, and the dark, brownish ground colour of the forewing.

WHERE Throughout the Alps, in the Pyrenees and mountains of Italy and eastern Europe, at altitudes from 900 to 2,500 m or more.

WHEN A late species, flying from the end of July to September.

LOOKALIKES

The **Marbled Ringlet** (*Erebia montana*) is very similar but both sexes usually have the veins on the underside hindwings narrowly outlined in white, and the females have brown-and-white laddered wing fringes.

Autumn Ringlet

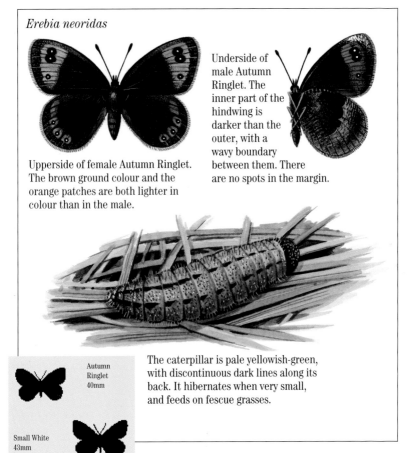

Erebia neoridas

Upperside of female Autumn Ringlet. The brown ground colour and the orange patches are both lighter in colour than in the male.

Underside of male Autumn Ringlet. The inner part of the hindwing is darker than the outer, with a wavy boundary between them. There are no spots in the margin.

Autumn Ringlet 40mm

Small White 43mm

The caterpillar is pale yellowish-green, with discontinuous dark lines along its back. It hibernates when very small, and feeds on fescue grasses.

This medium-sized ringlet has a more compact, rounded wing shape than other ringlets, and is distinguished by the shape of the strongly tapering yellow-orange patches on the forewing, and the flat outer edges of the black-centred orange spots near the margin of the hindwings. The female underside is similar to that of the male, but paler. The butterflies inhabit mountain slopes at medium altitudes, often associated with bare rocks, on which the males bask with wings spread, facing the morning sun. Later they become more active, males seeking out females. Like many other ringlets, the males commonly drink fluid from patches of damp ground, or in cracks among the rocks on which they settle. Both sexes visit flowers such as eyebright, scabious, hawkbit and ragworts, when they are easy to approach for photography.

A male Autumn Ringlet basks on a rocky slope. Note the wide, tapering orange bands on the forewings, and the distinctive shape of the orange spots on the hindwings. The males emerge up to two weeks earlier than the females.

WHERE The butterfly has a discontinuous distribution in the mountains of southern France, the Pyrenees and Italy, occurring at altitudes from 500 to 1,600 m.

WHEN This is a late-flying species that can be seen from the beginning of August through to early October.

LOOKALIKES

The shapes of the orange patches on the fore- and hindwings are distinctive. The unusually late flight period also helps with identification.

Bright-eyed Ringlet

Erebia oeme

Upperside of male Bright-eyed Ringlet. The male is very dark brown, with two bright 'eye' spots in each forewing, and another row of them on the hindwing. The pattern is repeated on the underside.

Underside of female Bright-eyed Ringlet. This is paler brown than the male. Note the black tips to the antennae (see lookalikes).

The caterpillar is pale greenish or yellowish with fine darker longitudinal lines. Its food plants include several grasses and sedges. The winter is spent in this stage.

Bright-eyed Ringlet 37mm

Small White 43mm

Like some other ringlets, this is a very variable butterfly and this can make for difficulty in identifying it. The reddish rings around the male 'eye' spots can form larger patches, or be almost absent in some populations. The butterflies inhabit lush, damp mountain meadows and marshy areas with long grasses or sedges from 1,600 m up to 2,500. In wet weather they hide deep in vegetation, but come up to bask with open wings when the sunshine returns - it is under these conditions that the 'eye' markings shine particularly brightly. They drink nectar from a wide range of flowers, but seem particularly attracted to yellow flowers in the dandelion family. At higher altitudes the caterpillars take two full seasons to complete their development. The chrysalis is pale cream-yellow with darker stripes and spots.

This female is warming up by basking in sunshine after a rainstorm. Notice the bright, shining white centres to the 'eye' spots. The males are darker with smaller, but still bright, 'eye' spots.

WHERE This species is widely distributed in European mountains: the Pyrenees, Massif Central, and the alpine range through to the Balkans.

WHEN The butterflies are on the wing from mid-June to mid-August, depending on locality.

LOOKALIKES

The bright 'eye' spots, and the underside hindwing, unmarked except for a row of orange-ringed 'eye' spots, separate it from most others. It has black tips to its antennae (see under **Woodland Ringlet**, page 198).

Piedmont Ringlet

Erebia meolans

Forewing of Piedmont Ringlet with three apical 'eye' spots.

Male upperside of Piedmont Ringlet. The male is darker brown than the female, and the band enclosing the variable 'eye' spots on the forewing is also darker red, and often broken.

Male underside of Piedmont Ringlet. This is very dark - almost black - with a slightly paler greyish area on the outer part of the hindwing. This contains three very small 'eye' spots.

Forewing of de Prunner's with three 'eye' spots in alignment.

Piedmont Ringlet 45mm

Small White 43mm

The caterpillar may be green or brownish, with a prominent darker line along the back.

This is another very variable species. Larger and more brightly marked specimens can be found in the mountains of Spain and the Pyrenees, whilst in the eastern Alps smaller forms, with reduced orange-red markings, predominate. The underside of the female is paler brown than that of the male, often with an ill-defined whitish boundary to the outer section of the hindwing, and orange-ringed eye spots. The Piedmont is one of the commonest and most widespread of the ringlets, and occurs from 600 up to 2,000 m, but most commonly around 900 to 1,100 m. It inhabits a wide range of grassy habitats including woodland clearings and the edges of tracks, as well as open grassy slopes and meadows. Both sexes frequently visit flowers for nectar, but the males are particularly fond of drinking moisture from bare rocks or soil.

A female settles with its wings open to bask in morning sunshine. It is similar to the Bright-eyed Ringlet, but the 'eye' markings are larger, and set in a wider orange band on the forewing.

WHERE The butterfly is widespread on most of the mountain ranges of southern Europe, including the Pyrenees, Massif Central, Alps, Jura, Vosges and the Appenines.

WHEN Depending on locality it may be seen from the beginning of June through to mid-August.

LOOKALIKES

Some forms are similar to the **Bright-eyed Ringlet. De Prunner's Ringlet** is also similar. It has three 'eye' spots near the apex of each forewing, and these are in alignment.

Dewy Ringlet

Erebia pandrose

Underside of male Dewy Ringlet. The silver-grey ground colour of the hindwing is distinctive, with its wavy black lines and finer black flecks.

Underside of male False Dewy Ringlet. Note the absence of black lines across the hindwing.

Dewy Ringlet
40 mm

Small White
43mm

The caterpillar of the Dewy Ringlet is usually green, with a dark line along the back, and discontinuous lines along its sides.

The ground colour of the upperside is paler in the female. In both sexes there is a row of two to four black spots in the ill-defined orange band on each forewing, and there are variable wavy darker lines running across the wings. There is often a row of red-ringed spots on the hindwing, but these are sometimes absent (as in the photo opposite). The butterfly inhabits wet grasslands and bogs in mountains, but occurs at lower altitudes in the northern part of its range. It sometimes visits flowers, but more often sips moisture from damp ground or mosses. It has a slow, flapping, 'lazy' flight, but is deceptively difficult to approach. The caterpillars feed on mat grass, fescues and other grasses, and take two years to complete their development.

This male is basking in sunshine among mosses and dwarf sallows in a Lapland bog. More southerly populations tend to have more spots on both fore- and hindwings. The flight is usually slow and close to the ground, but swift and zigzagging when disturbed.

WHERE A discontinuous distribution, including the east Pyrenees, the Alps, and mountains of the Balkans and eastern Europe in the southern range, and also in Norway, Sweden and Finland.

WHEN In its southern range it flies from early June until August, but in Lapland not until July.

LOOKALIKES

The **False Dewy Ringlet** (*Erebia sthennyo*) is very localised in the Pyrenees. The underside hindwings lack the black wavy lines present in the Dewy Ringlet (see paintings opposite).

Ringlet

Aphantopus hyperantus

Underside of a male: dark grey-brown (paler in the female), with a series of yellow-ringed and white-centred eye spots.

Underside of *arete* form: the underside spots are variable. In this extreme form, they are reduced to tiny white points.

The fully grown caterpillar is pale brown with a black stripe along its back and pale white and pink stripes along its sides. It feeds on grasses at night.

Ringlet
40 mm

Small White
43mm

The upperside is uniformly dark brown – almost black in freshly emerged males. There is a variable row of black 'eye' spots on each wing, which are usually better defined and white-centred in the females. Freshly emerged specimens have a distinctive white fringe to the wings. Ringlets are sometimes found along overgrown hedgerows and scrubby meadows, but they are most commonly sighted in damp woodland rides and clearings where grasses are allowed to grow long. The flight is usually quite slow and feeble, and the males frequently bask with open wings on a prominent perch. In dull weather they settle with their wings closed. The female flies low among the grasses, scattering her eggs as she flies. They visit a wide range of flowers for nectar, but are particularly attracted to bramble.

A male is feeding on St. John's Wort in a woodland ride. Note the rather obscure 'eye' spots and the white fringe round the wing edges. Females are paler brown and often have larger 'eye' spots with yellow rings around them.

WHERE Very widespread lowland butterfly in western and central Europe, but is absent from most of Iberia, Italy, Greece and northern Scandinavia.

WHEN On the wing though July and into the first half of August.

LOOKALIKES

In flight it can resemble the **Meadow Brown** (*Maniola jurtina*), but the white fringes are unmistakable in fresh specimens, as is the distinctive underside pattern.

Meadow Brown

Maniola jurtina

Upperside of male Meadow Brown.

The underside of a male Meadow Brown. The spots on the hindwing vary in number.

Underside of female Dusky Meadow Brown (see lookalikes). Note the extra 'eye' spot on the forewing.

When fully grown the caterpillar is bright green with a darker green stripe along its back, and a paler one along its sides. It has fine white hairs, and feeds nocturnally on grasses.

Meadow Brown 45-50 mm

Small White 43mm

This is one of the most familiar and widespread of all the European butterflies. In unimproved lowland grasslands they can occur in huge numbers, flying up in clouds as they are disturbed by passers-by. However, agricultural change has restricted them to uncultivated habitats such as ex-industrial sites, roadside verges and country parks. The males are dark brown, with a small, yellow-ringed 'eye' spot and a band of scent scales on each forewing. The females are larger and more brightly coloured than the males - Linnaeus even considered them a different species. Both sexes are active, even in cloudy weather, basking with open wings to warm up, or flying low over their grassland habitat. The females feed from flowers more often than do the males.

A female Meadow Brown drinks nectar from thistle flowers. Note the wide yellow-orange patches on her forewings. There are several variant forms in Europe, some with very extensive yellow markings in the females.

WHERE Found throughout Europe except for northern Scandinavia, inhabiting meadows, roadside verges, hedgerows and other open spaces.

WHEN Adults fly from early June (earlier in southern Europe) until September. In hot countries they have a summer resting period.

LOOKALIKES

Dusky (*Hyponephele lycaon*) and **Oriental Meadow Browns** (*H. lupina*) occur in southern and eastern parts of Europe, differing mainly in the pattern of spots, and the shape of the band of scent scales in the males. See also **Ringlet** (page 206).

Gatekeeper

Maniola (Pyronia) tithonus

Upperside of female Gatekeeper. Note the large orange patches on the wings, and the 'eye' spots towards the tips of the forewings.

The underside hindwing has a variegated brown and yellowish pattern, with a few small white-centred spots. The forewing resembles the upperside.

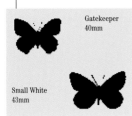

The fully grown caterpillar is either pale grey-brown or pale green, with darker stripes along its back and sides. The winter is spent as a small caterpillar, which then feeds on grassblades in spring and early summer.

Gatekeeper
40mm

Small White
43mm

The chrysalis is formed among vegetation close to the ground. It is pale grey-brown with dark brown striations on the wing covers and other dark markings.

The Gatekeeper is a medium-sized butterfly of rough grassland, close-ly associated with shrubs, hedges or woodland-edge. In many areas its habitat has been lost due to agricultural intensification but it remains widespread and often common in neglected field edges, lane sides, uncultivated land and urban open spaces (including domestic gardens). The males perch on prominent branches of shrubs, where they bask with open wings, awaiting females. Both sexes spend much of their time imbibing nectar from hedgerow flowers such as knapweeds, fleabane and ragworts, but they are especially attracted to bramble blossom. Eggs are laid singly on or near the fine grasses such as bents and meadow grasses on which the caterpillars feed. In laying their eggs they choose longer grass in sunny locations close to shrubs or a hedge.

A male Gatekeeper perches on a bramble leaf, ready to dart out and intercept a passing female. Note the broad bands of scent scales cutting across the orange patches on the forewings.

WHERE The Gatekeeper is a widespread and common species throughout most of southern and central Europe, reaching as far north as the Scottish borders in Britain.

WHEN There is one generation each year, and the butterflies can be seen from July through to early September.

LOOKALIKES

The Southern (*M. cecilia*) and **Spanish** (*M. bathseba*) **Gatekeepers** occur in parts of southern Europe. The former is smaller, with more rounded wings, while the latter has a distinctive whitish streak across the underside hindwing.

Small Heath

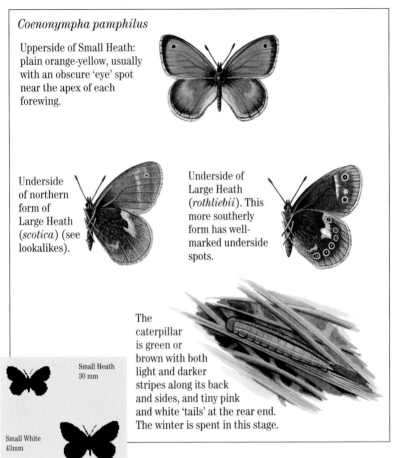

Coenonympha pamphilus

Upperside of Small Heath: plain orange-yellow, usually with an obscure 'eye' spot near the apex of each forewing.

Underside of northern form of Large Heath (*scotica*) (see lookalikes).

Underside of Large Heath (*rothliebii*). This more southerly form has well-marked underside spots.

The caterpillar is green or brown with both light and darker stripes along its back and sides, and tiny pink and white 'tails' at the rear end. The winter is spent in this stage.

Small Heath
30 mm

Small White
43mm

The Small Heath is the commonest and most widespread of a group of small, orange-brown coloured heath butterflies. However, the loss of its grassland sites through agricultural intensification has led to a decline in its population in several European countries, including Britain. Coastal dunes and grazing marshes, heaths, roadside verges and remaining unimproved pasture are its favoured habitats. The underside hindwing is also very variable in colour, but it is usually various shades of grey, darker towards the wing base, and often with an ill-defined pale patch around the middle of the wing (see photograph). There are usually tiny 'eye' spots towards the margin of the hindwing. The butterflies rest with wings closed, but open them briefly during courtship. There are two or more generations each year.

Small Heaths always settle with their wings closed. Males gather together to attract females, which fly off after mating to lay their eggs on fine wild grasses such as bents and fescues.

WHERE Throughout Europe, reaching as far north as northern Scandinavia, in unimproved grassland on well-drained soils.

WHEN Adults fly from early June (earlier in southern Europe) until September. In hot countries they have a summer resting period.

LOOKALIKES

Most of the other heath butterflies have more clearly marked underside hindwings, with well-defined 'eye' spots. Northern populations of the **Large Heath** (*Coenonympha tullia*) are very similar, but can usually be distinguished by size and habitat.

Pearly Heath/Chestnut Heath

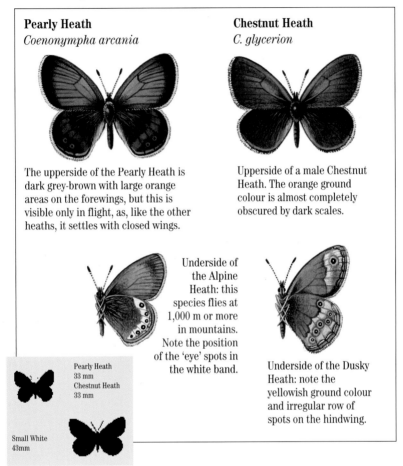

Pearly Heath
Coenonympha arcania

Chestnut Heath
C. glycerion

The upperside of the Pearly Heath is dark grey-brown with large orange areas on the forewings, but this is visible only in flight, as, like the other heaths, it settles with closed wings.

Upperside of a male Chestnut Heath. The orange ground colour is almost completely obscured by dark scales.

Underside of the Alpine Heath: this species flies at 1,000 m or more in mountains. Note the position of the 'eye' spots in the white band.

Underside of the Dusky Heath: note the yellowish ground colour and irregular row of spots on the hindwing.

Pearly Heath
33 mm
Chestnut Heath
33 mm

Small White
43mm

The **Pearly Heath** occupies a wide variety of habitats, from open grassland to glades and rides in woodland. The distinctive underside hindwings have a series of prominent 'eye' spots set around a broad whitish band. The furthest forward of these spots is set at the inner edge of the white band.

The **Chestnut Heath** is another grassland species, but it can additionally be found in light woodland and scrub, as well as in subalpine meadows up to 1,800 m or more. The row of 'eye' spots on the underside hindwing is very variable: sometimes strongly marked, as in Spain and the Pyrenees, sometimes virtually absent at high altitudes in mountains. The triangular white mark is a constant feature. In some forms there is a bright orange line along the wing margins on the underside.

*A **Pearly Heath** hides in shrubs during poor weather. Note the position of the 'eye' spot at the front edge of the hindwing.*

*A **Chestnut Heath** seeking nectar from a sage (*Salvia species*) flower. Notice the small triangular white mark on the hindwing.*

WHERE AND WHEN Widespread through western and central Europe, but absent from Britain. Flies May to August.

Pearly Heath

Chestnut Heath

WHERE AND WHEN Widespread in western and central Europe, but absent from Britain. Flies June to August.

Speckled Wood

Pararge aegeria

Underside of *tircis* form. The mottled underside pattern gives excellent camouflage when the butterfly is at rest.

Upperside of typical form of Speckled Wood, *aegeria*. Note the orange spots, and the dark band of scent scales in this male specimen.

The fully grown caterpillar is green, with a darker line along its back, and pale, lime-green to yellow lines along its sides. It feeds on several species of woodland grasses.

The compact chrysalis is green or brownish with white points on its back. The winter may be spent as either caterpillar or chrysalis.

Speckled Wood 40 mm

Small White 43mm

There are two clearly distinct forms of the Speckled Wood in Europe. The typical form is dark brown with bright orange spots, and an 'eye' marking near the apex of each forewing. The hindwing has a row of orange patches with 'eye' markings in the outer part of the wing. The underside hindwing has a mottled pattern with wavy cross lines. The form *tircis*, which occurs in Britain, parts of France, northern Europe and the Balkans, is similar, but the orange is replaced by pale yellow-cream. The Speckled Wood is associated with mature woodland, where the males occupy territories in dappled sun spots. They fly out from a prominent perch to chase off other insects and intercept passing females. Both sexes feed from aphid honeydew on leaves, and visit flowers less frequently than do most butterflies.

A female of form tircis *rests between bouts of egg laying in its woodland habitat. The males have smaller pale spots, and a dark band of scent scales on each forewing.*

WHERE Throughout Europe, including southern Scandinavia. Recently expanded its range in Britain and other northern countries, and can be found along hedges, in urban gardens and parks as well as woodland.

WHEN Several cycles in a year. May be seen from March through to October, depending on climate and locality.

LOOKALIKES

The only truly similar species fly in Madeira and the Canaries. The **Wall Brown** (see page 228) has a different wing shape and more extensive orange spaces on the wings.

Wall Brown

Pararge (Lasiommata) megera

Upperside of male. Notice the dark band of scent scales on the forewing.

The underside is visible when the butterfly is at rest or sheltering in dull weather. The hindwing is grey with darker zigzag lines and a row of 'eye' markings.

The fully grown caterpillar is green with fine whitish longitudinal lines. It feeds at night on grasses, and spends the winter in this stage.

Wall Brown
40 mm

Small White
43mm

The Wall Brown is a butterfly of nutrient-poor grassland, usually where vegetation cover is sparse and broken. It frequently basks in sun spots on rocks or bare ground, and favours hot microclimates. Both sexes have a regular pattern of yellow-orange patches, separated by a network of dark brown bands. When at rest or sheltering in dull weather the wings are closed, so that only the underside is visible. The forewings are raised to display the 'eye' markings when the butterfly is alarmed, but when the forewings are dropped out of sight, the grey hindwings give excellent camouflage against tree trunks or rocks in the background. Males hold territories on rocks or by track sides . Here they sit with wings half open on rocks or by the edge of paths, flitting up and settling again a few metres further on when disturbed.

A female Wall Brown basks in bright sunshine on a dead branch. Note the dark lines running down from the leading edge of the forewing. Pale forms of the Large Wall Brown have one less.

WHERE Wherever there is suitable habitat throughout Europe, absent only from northern Scandinavia and parts of northern Britain. Mainly a coastal species in southern and central Britain in recent years.

WHEN Depending on locality, may be seen from April through to October, flying in two or three generations.

LOOKALIKES

The **Large Wall Brown** (see page 230) usually has a darker ground colour, and pale forms have fewer cross bands on the forewing. The **Northern Wall Brown** (*Lasiommata petropolitana*) has a dark brown ground colour. See also **Speckled Wood** (page 226).

Large Wall Brown

Pararge (Lasiommata) maera

Upperside of male Large Wall Brown. Notice the dark band of scent scales across the forewing.

Underside of Large Wall Brown. The 'eye' spots are usually larger and more prominent than in the Wall Brown.

Upperside of male Northern Wall Brown. Note the faint wavy line across the hindwing.

The caterpillar is green with both darker green and yellowish lines along its body. It feeds on grassblades, and spends the winter in this stage.

Large Wall Brown
45-48 mm

Small White
43mm

The Large Wall Brown inhabits a wide variety of habitats, including grassy areas, light woodland and scrub. However, it is usually associated with exposed rocks or bare ground facing the sun. The males are particularly inclined to settle on rock faces or scree with wings wide open, basking in the sun. They are strongly territorial and fly up to intercept passing insects. They are easily disturbed, but usually settle again, nearby, and later return to a favoured sun spot. The females visit flowers more frequently, and they are particularly attracted to thistles, scabious and knapweeds. The underside is similar to the Wall Brown, but with larger 'eye' markings. The wing fringes are laddered brown and white. In southern Europe, the *adrasta* form has a mainly orange ground colour, which bears a resemblance to the Wall Brown.

This female Large Wall Brown is the typical Central European form. At high altitudes and in northern Europe the orange markings can be much reduced, but in the south the females can be quite similar to the Wall Brown in colour.

WHERE Very widespread in Europe, but is absent from Britain and northern Scandinavia.

WHEN In the southern part of its range it completes two generations in a year, and can be seen from April to October. In the north it flies from June to August, but is most frequent in July.

LOOKALIKES

Form *adrasta* resembles the **Wall Brown** (see page 228). The **Northern Wall Brown** (see painting opposite) flies in northern Europe and at high altitudes in mountains. It is usually smaller and has a wavy line across the upperside hindwing.

Grizzled Skipper

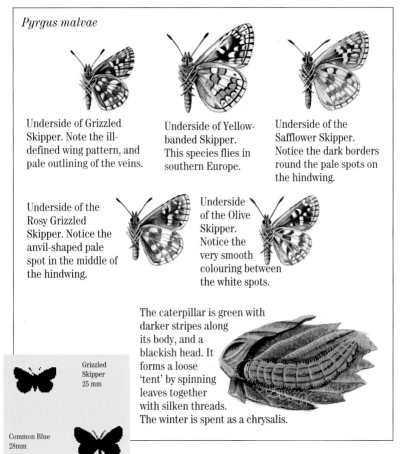

Pyrgus malvae

Underside of Grizzled Skipper. Note the ill-defined wing pattern, and pale outlining of the veins.

Underside of Yellow-banded Skipper. This species flies in southern Europe.

Underside of the Safflower Skipper. Notice the dark borders round the pale spots on the hindwing.

Underside of the Rosy Grizzled Skipper. Notice the anvil-shaped pale spot in the middle of the hindwing.

Underside of the Olive Skipper. Notice the very smooth colouring between the white spots.

The caterpillar is green with darker stripes along its body, and a blackish head. It forms a loose 'tent' by spinning leaves together with silken threads. The winter is spent as a chrysalis.

Grizzled Skipper 25 mm

Common Blue 28mm

The Grizzled Skipper is one of the most widespread of fifteen similar European species. The black or grey upperside with a chessboard pattern of white spots is shared by the whole group of butterflies. The pattern on the underside is similar, but paler. In the Grizzled Skipper the underside pattern is indistinct, but the veins on the hindwing are highlighted with whitish scales. The butterflies inhabit flowery grassland, such as unimproved meadows, downland slopes, wide and sunny woodland rides, railway cuttings and former industrial sites. They frequently settle on a favoured perch in the sun, or visit wild flowers such as bugle or bird's-foot trefoil. The eggs are laid on wild strawberry, creeping cinquefoil and other related plants. Their flight low over the ground is sudden and very fast.

This male Grizzled Skipper has settled to drink nectar from a flower. Notice the long, narrow pouch formed by the rolling back of the leading edge of the forewing. This contains the scent scales, used in attracting females.

WHERE Widespread throughout Europe, but absent from northern Britain and northern Scandinavia. It has declined in a number of European countries, particularly in southern Britain.

WHEN Usually one generation, on the wing April to June, and a second may fly in July and August.

LOOKALIKES

Many lookalikes; see paintings opposite for examples of some of the more distinctive members of the group.

Red Underwing Skipper

Spialia sertorius

Upperside of Red Underwing Skipper. Note the row of tiny white spots around the wing margins. The wing fringes are noticeably laddered black and white.

Underside of the Orbed Red-underwing Skipper. Note the rounded shapes of the white spots.

The caterpillar is dark brown with a pale band along its back, and has long, pale hairs. It shelters in a 'tent' of leaves during the day.

Red Underwing Skipper 24 mm

Common Blue 28mm

The Red Underwing Skipper inhabits hot, dry habitats with abundant wild flowers. It is found in Mediterranean scrubland, unimproved meadows, roadside verges and clearings in light woodland. It is very small, and has the sudden, darting flight typical of skipper butterflies. The most distinctive feature is the underside hindwing. This is a rich red with contrasting white spots. The butterflies spend much of their time resting in the sun on bare ground or rocks, with wings half open, or visiting a wide variety of flowers for nectar. Mating pairs can often be seen perched on flower heads or other vegetation. The females lay their eggs on salad burnet, and probably on other related plants. The resulting caterpillars feed at night and the winter is spent in this stage.

A male Red Underwing Skipper alights briefly on a flower head. The brick-red underside, small size and low, rapid flight are distinctive.

WHERE Widespread throughout central and southern Europe, but absent from Britain and Scandinavia, from sea level to altitudes of 2,000 m. or more in mountains.

WHEN In most localities there are two generations in a year, the first flying from late April to June, and the second in July and August.

LOOKALIKES

The **Orbed Red-underwing Skipper** (*Spialia orbifer*) occurs in south eastern Europe. The spots on its underside are rounded.

Mallow Skipper

Carcharodus alceae

Upperside of female Mallow Skipper. Note the small whitish spots on the forewings, and the ill-defined bands across the hindwings.

Upperside of Marbled Skipper. Note the larger white spots on the forewings and white band across each hindwing.

Underside of Tufted Marbled Skipper. Note the elongated white marginal markings on the hindwing.

Underside of Mallow Skipper. Note the small and ill-defined spots on the hindwing.

Underside of the Southern Marbled Skipper. Note the well-defined white bands across the hindwing.

Mallow Skipper 30 mm

Common Blue 28mm

The Mallow Skipper is the most widespread of a small group of mainly southern skipper butterflies. They favour hot, dry habitats, where they settle for long periods on bare ground or flower heads absorbing the sun's heat. The males frequently dart off in pursuit of females or other insects, usually returning to their favourite perch. Pheromones contained in a narrow pouch on the forewing (see the photograph opposite) are released by the male in a courtship flight. The females are less frequently observed, searching for suitable plants - mostly species of mallow - on which to lay their eggs. In the Mediterranean area, cultivated mallows in gardens are also used by this species. The ground colour is very variable – from light orange-brown (as in the photograph) to (more commonly) dark grey-brown, with paler areas that often have a pink or violet tint.

A male Mallow Skipper basks on a flower head. Note the scalloped edges to the hindwings, and the small whitish semi-transparent spots on the forewings. The leading edge of each forewing is rolled back to form a pouch that contains scent scales.

WHERE Widespread and often common throughout central and southern Europe, but is absent from Britain and the north.

WHEN Depending on locality and season, it can complete three or more generations in a year, and can be seen from April through to October.

LOOKALIKES

The **Southern Marbled**, (*Carcharodus boeticus*) **Marbled** (*C. lavatherae*) and **Tufted Marbled** skippers (*C. flocciferus*) are similar. See the paintings opposite.

Dingy Skipper

Erynnis tages

The underside of the Dingy Skipper is much paler than the upperside, often with a slightly yellowish tint, and variable rows of tiny pale points. The butterflies rarely settle with wings closed, but typically have a more moth-like pose when at rest.

Upperside of Burnet Companion Moth (see lookalikes). This day-flying moth often occurs in the same habitats as the Dingy Skipper, and looks quite similar.

The caterpillar forms a loose shelter of leaves on its food plant, and goes into hibernation in mid-July. When fully grown it is green with a black head.

The chrysalis is formed in the hibernation shelter in early spring. It is brown, with a green head and green wing covers.

Dingy Skipper 28 mm

Common Blue 28mm

This small brown butterfly could easily be overlooked, but on closer examination the fine whitish patterning on the upperside is very pleasing to the eye. The butterflies inhabit open, sunny habitats with plenty of wild flowers – particularly bird's-foot trefoil, on which their eggs are laid. They require a mixture of short, sparse turf, with patches of bare ground, on which they often bask in sunny weather, and which can also be colonized by their food plant. Nearby tall vegetation is also required for shelter and for roosting at night. Open woodland rides, old quarries, disused railway lines and downland slopes are typical habitats. In several European countries, habitats have been lost due to a combination of more intensive use of agricultural and wasteland and lack of management of other sites, leading to the shading out of the bird's-foot trefoil.

A pair of Dingy Skippers mating on a low birch twig. Note the curled back leading edge of the forewing in the male. This is the source of the pheromones he uses in the courtship flight.

WHERE Widespread throughout Europe, except for the northern part of Scandinavia.

WHEN In the northern part of its range, usually one generation a year, with adults flying in May and early June. In favourable seasons, and in southern Europe there is a partial second generation in July and August.

LOOKALIKES

Apart from the very localised **Inky Skipper** (*Erynnis marloyi*) of south-eastern Europe, there are no similar butterflies. However, it could be confused with the **Burnet Companion Moth** (*Euclida gryphica*) (see the painting opposite).

Chequered Skipper

Carterocephalus palaemon

Underside of Chequered Skipper. The underside is usually not seen except when the butterfly closes its wings at night or in dull weather. The forewing repeats the pattern of the upperside, but in more subdued hues.

The caterpillar is green when small, but turns yellowish, with red-brown stripes when fully grown. It forms a shelter by spinning together the edges of a grassblade and feeds on various grass species, especially bromes and purple moor grass. The winter is spent in this stage.

Chequered Skipper
26 mm

The chrysalis is formed in spring in a 'tent' of grassblades, and is pale buff, with darker stripes along its body.

Common Blue
28mm

The main habitats for this butterfly are open, grassy and damp areas in woodland. The practices of coppicing and maintenance of wide, sunny rides have been important in providing suitable conditions, but as they have been abandoned in many areas in favour of conifer plantation, the butterfly has declined. In Britain it was once quite common in the English Midlands, but is now confined to western Scotland. The males settle on prominent perches, from which they fly out to chase off other butterflies or court passing females, usually returning to the same spot. The females are less often seen, and spend more of their time seeking nectar from flowers or flying among the lush grasses on which they lay their eggs. As with the other skippers, the flight is very rapid, but they are relatively easy to approach when at rest.

A male on a favoured perch in a Swedish bog. The chequered forewing pattern of orange-yellow angular spots on a dark brown background is distinctive. The hindwing's central spots are rounded, and there is a row of tiny yellowish points round the wing margins.

WHERE Widespread across central and western Europe from sea level up to altitudes of 1,600 m, but localised in northern Scandinavia, and rare in Britain. It is absent from most of southern Europe.

WHEN One generation each year, with adults flying from mid-May through June, or later at high altitudes.

LOOKALIKES

The female of the **Northern Chequered Skipper** is very similar (see page 244).

Large Chequered Skipper

Heteropterus morpheus

Upperside of male.
The pattern of
dark, blackish
brown with small,
bright splashes of
yellow on the
forewings is distinctive.
The female is very
similar, but the wings are
more rounded. The wing fringes are
laddered brown/black-and-white in both
sexes.

The pale green chrysalis
is attached to a
grassblade, and
formed in late
spring.

The caterpillar
lives in a shelter formed, as in the Chequered Skipper,
by spinning the edges of a
grassblade together. When
fully grown, it is green with
a dark stripe along its back
and paler ones along its
sides. The winter is spent in
this stage.

Large
Chequered
Skipper
34 mm

Common Blue
28mm

The typical habitat for this butterfly is open glades and rides in damp woodland, but it also can be found in more open damp, scrubby heaths and wetlands. The males are more frequently seen than the females, as they fly low over long grasses with a distinctive 'looping' flight. When engaged in this behaviour they rarely rest and can be difficult to approach for photography. When they do settle on a grassblade or flower head, they usually sit with their wings closed, showing the brightly-patterned underside hindwing. Occasionally, however, they open their wings briefly to bask. In hot, dry weather they sometimes gather in large numbers to drink fluid from puddles or damp soil. In several parts of Europe this butterfly is threatened by drainage of wetlands and intensive forest management. The eggs are laid on the stems of various grasses, including brome, moor grass and reeds.

A male Large Chequered Skipper sips nectar. The large, black-bordered white spots against the pale yellow background are distinctive. The tip of the forewing is just visible, and has a similar pattern, but the rest of the underside forewing is dark brown.

WHERE A rather scattered distribution across western and eastern Europe; absent from Britain, almost all of Scandinavia and the far south.

WHEN Just one generation each year, with the adults flying from late June through July.

LOOKALIKES

When flying, the contrasting upper- and underside markings, showing the alternate pale and dark faces of the wings, are unique, as is its looping flight.

Northern Chequered Skipper

Carterocephalus silvicolus

Upperside of female. The chequered orange-yellow and brown pattern is similar to that of the Chequered Skipper (see lookalikes), and the two can easily be mistaken as they often fly together where their ranges overlap in northern Europe. Note the way the outer row of spots is fused together on the forewing.

Underside of the Northern Chequered Skipper.

The caterpillar lives in a shelter formed, as in the Chequered Skipper, by spinning the edges of a grassblade together. When fully grown, it is green with a dark stripe along its back and paler ones along its sides. The winter is spent in this

The chrysalis is formed among grass stems and is yellow-green with narrow reddish stripes along its back.

Northern Chequered Skipper 28 mm

Common Blue 28mm

The Northern Chequered Skipper inhabits damp woodland glades, forest edges, and road and track sides through forests, as well as in flowery meadows close to woodland. In the far north they fly in forests around marshes. The males spend much of their time resting with open wings on prominent perches among tall grasses. Their golden-yellow wings gleam in the sunlight, making them very easy to spot. They tend to remain on their perch even when the sun goes in, but slowly close their wings. They are not difficult to approach for photography, but when disturbed they fly extremely quickly and soon disappear from view. The females are less brilliantly coloured than the males, and spend much of their time among grasses laying eggs or visiting flowers for nectar. Both sexes are strongly attracted to the flowers of wood cranesbill.

A male drinks from wood cranesbill in a forest meadow. The golden-yellow forewings shimmer in the light, especially if the butterfly has just emerged. The black forewing spots may be smaller, and the hind wings often have a yellow sheen over their dark scales.

WHERE North-eastern Europe, from northern Germany to Finland and Scandinavia, becoming very localised in northern Norway.

WHEN One generation each year, with adults flying from late May to the end of June.

LOOKALIKES

The males are quite distinctive, but the females are similar to the **Chequered Skipper** (page 240). In the Northern Chequered Skipper the orange-yellow forewing spots are larger, and the outer ones are fused together to form an irregular band.

Lulworth Skipper

Thymelicus acteon

The underside is revealed when the butterfly closes its wings at night, and in dull weather when it takes shelter among the grasses. It is orange-brown and unmarked, except for a faint 'echo' of the pale rays in the females and the scent mark in the males. Often there is a greenish suffusion, especially in the males.

The chrysalis is attached by silken threads low down on a grass stem or leaf. It is green, with a small projection at the head end.

The caterpillar lives in the shelter of a tube formed by spinning together the edges of a grassblade. In England Tor-grass only is used, but further south the caterpillars feed on other grasses, including bromes and common couch. The fully grown caterpillar is green with a darker green stripe along its back and pale ones along its sides. The head is beige-brown. It hibernates soon after hatching from the egg.

Lulworth Skipper 26 mm

Common Blue 28mm

The Lulworth Skipper is a butterfly of hot, dry grassland slopes, with abundant flowers and long, coarse grasses. The typical resting posture in sunny weather is shown in the photograph: forewings half spread, and the hindwings below almost flat. The ground colour is darker than the bright orange-brown of the other skippers in this group, and the females are distinctive with the arc of pale patches on their forewings. The females prefer to lay their eggs on clumps of tall grass, so, unlike many other grass-land butterflies, this one has benefited from abandonment of grazing in some areas, and the decline of rabbit populations. Where conditions are favourable colonies can build up huge populations of as many as 100,000 individuals. They fly only when the sun shines, but spend much of their time visiting downland flowers or basking, and are easily approached.

A female Lulworth Skipper rests on a seed-head. Note the distinctive 'rays' of paler colour on her forewing. These are lacking in the male, which has a diagonal line of black scent-scales on its forewing, similar to the Small Skipper.

WHERE Widespread throughout southern and central Europe, but absent from the north. Occurs on the southern coast of Britain, close to the northern limit of its European range.

WHEN One generation a year; a long flight period from May (in the south) to late September (in England). Most abundant in August.

LOOKALIKES

The **Small** (see page 248) and **Essex** (*Thymelicus lineola*) **Skippers** are closely related and similar in appearance, but the darker ground colour in the males, and the arc of paler spots on the female upperside are distinctive. See also **Large Skipper** (page 250).

Small Skipper

Thymelicus sylvestris

Upperside of female Small Skipper. Note the dark borders to the wings, and fine black outlining of the veins.

The upperside of male Essex Skipper (see lookalikes). Note the shorter scent band, which runs parallel to the leading edge of the forewing.

The tip of the antenna in the Essex Skipper is black, with a sharp edge, looking as if it's dipped in ink. The Small Skipper's antenna tip can be dark, but lacks the sharp edge.

Underside of Small Skipper. The underside is orange-brown, with a pale grey-green suffusion.

Caterpillars hibernate as a small group, and disperse in the spring. They make a tubular shelter of a grassblade and feed on the grass through the spring and early summer. The fully grown caterpillar is pale green, with darker green longitudinal stripes and a green head.

Small Skipper 28 mm

Common Blue 28mm

The Small Skipper is one of the most familiar of the European butterflies, and can be seen wherever wild grasses are allowed to grow long: in old or abandoned meadows, rough, uncultivated grassland, ex-industrial sites in towns, on roadside verges and hedgerows, grassy rides in woodland, sea defences and many other places. The males are territorial, perching on prominent vegetation, and flying up to intercept passing females. Both sexes bask in sunshine with forewings half spread in the typical posture of this group of skippers. Mating takes place on the tops of vegetation or among the tall grasses. They frequently visit flowers such as knapweeds, burdocks, black horehound and creeping thistle for nectar. Although, like the other skippers, they can fly very fast, they rarely go long distances and are easily approached for photography.

A male Small Skipper favours a flower head of bell heather as its perch. Note the long, well-defined scent band on the forewing. It is set slightly diagonally to the leading edge of the wing and reaches back towards the rear edge.

WHERE Common and widespread throughout Europe but is absent from the north (Norway, Sweden and Finland, and northern Britain).

WHEN One generation each year, most commonly seen through July and early August, but in favourable localities may start to fly as early as the end of May.

LOOKALIKES

The **Essex Skipper** (*Thymelicus lineola*) has clear black tips to its antennae, best seen from in front, and slightly below. The scent band in the male is shorter and placed differently (see paintings opposite). The **Lulworth Skipper** is also similar (see page 246).

Large Skipper/Silver-spotted Skipper

Large Skipper
Ochlodes venatus (sylvanus)

Silver-spotted Skipper
Hesperia comma

Upperside of male Large Skipper. Note the dark wing borders enclosing orange-yellow spots near the apex of the forewing.

Underside of Large Skipper. The pattern of orange-yellow spots on the upperside is repeated, but more faintly, on the underside. These spots are never so clear and bright as in the Silver-spotted Skipper.

Upperside of male Silver-spotted Skipper: the pattern on the upperside is very similar to that of the Large Skipper, but the pale spots near the apex of the forewing are yellow and contrast more strongly with the dark border.

When fully grown the caterpillar of the Large Skipper is blue-green with a darker green stripe along its back, paler cream-coloured stripes down its sides and a dark brown head. It feeds on the blades of grasses such as cocksfoot and false brome.

Large Skipper
30-33 mm
Silver-spotted
Skipper
30-33 mm

Common Blue
28mm

The **Large Skipper** inhabits rough grassland with flowers in a wide variety of locations: roadside verges, open spaces in woods, hedgerows, ex-industrial sites and waste ground in towns. The species favours areas with tufts of long, coarse grasses often in the shade of shrubs or other tall vegetation. The males perch in the manner typical of this group of skippers, with forewings part-open.

The **Silver-spotted Skipper** is a butterfly of short, dry and sparse grassland, where sheep's fescue grass abounds. In the northern part of its range (including downland of southern England) it requires hot microclimates, and frequently basks on bare earth or stones provided by rabbit diggings. Behaviour otherwise resembles that of the Large Skipper, and it frequently visits flowers such as thyme and stemless thistle.

*A female **Large Skipper** sips nectar from a clover flower. Note the chessboard pattern of yellow and brown on the forewing.*

*A female **Silver-spotted Skipper** drinks nectar from a stemless thistle. The shining white spots on the underside are distinctive.*

WHERE AND WHEN
The Large Skipper occurs throughout Europe, including southern Scandinavia. Seen from May to early September, most common in early July.

Large Skipper

Silver-spotted Skipper

WHERE AND WHEN
The Silver-spotted Skipper is is more localised in the northern part of its range, but does occur in the far north of Scandinavia. It has a later flight period and is most common in August.

INDEX

Butterfly Conservation (see page 18)

Butterfly Conservation (www.butterfly-conservation.org) is a UK charity set up to monitor butterfly populations and work for their preservation. With partner organisations in several other European countries it has helped to set up Butterfly Conservation Europe (www.bc-europe.org).